TOSS

S

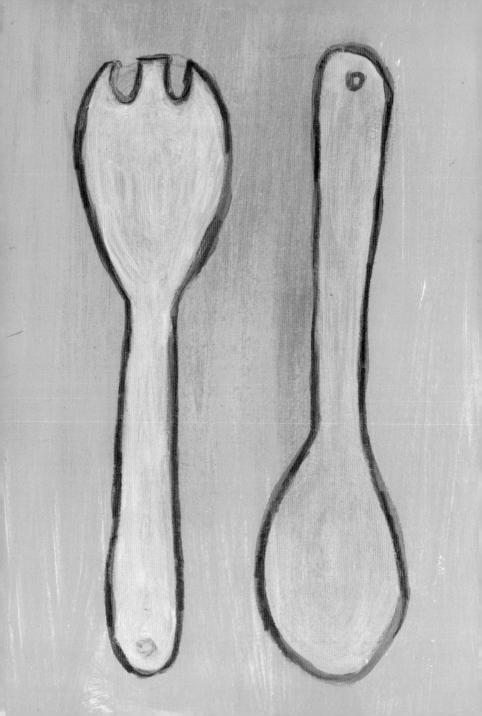

THE AUSTRALIAN
Women's Weekly

TOSS
salads + stir-fries

contents

A casual salad or stir-fry is truly the epitome of easy cooking – fresh produce and great ingredients tossed together in harmonious arrangement. It's quick, easy cooking that fits the bill for a tasty meal at the end of a working day. The idea of 'tossing' ingredients together sounds casual and unplanned, and that's how your dish should look. But if you want it to taste fabulous, you can't be flippant about which ingredients are tossed with which – a salad or a stir-fry shouldn't just be a repository for leftovers. Often less-is-more and a squeeze of lime can be enough to fine-tune a recipe to perfection. The trick to making these dishes special is care and attention to balance – of textures, flavours and selection of complementary elements. Crisp salad leaves with a creamy dressing or the sweet and salty components of a Thai stir-fry are a surprising and heavenly match. The recipes in this book make a casual salad or stir-fry a captivating ensemble of flavours. With a few fresh ingredients picked up on the way home from work and a pantry stocked with basic sauces, vinegars and oils you can produce brilliant results.

salads

Thai crab and mango salad

500g fresh crab meat
1 firm medium mango (430g)
100g mizuna
1 cup loosely packed fresh mint leaves
lime and chilli dressing
⅓ cup (80ml) lime juice
2 fresh long red chillies, sliced thinly
5cm piece fresh ginger (25g), cut into matchsticks
2 shallots (50g), sliced thinly
1 tablespoon fish sauce
2 tablespoons grated palm sugar
2 teaspoons peanut oil

1 Make lime and chilli dressing.
2 Combine crab in medium bowl with half the dressing.
3 Using vegetable peeler, slice mango into thin strips. Place mango in large bowl with mizuna, mint and remaining dressing; toss gently to combine.
4 Divide salad among serving plates; top with crab mixture.
lime and chilli dressing place ingredients in screw-top jar; shake well.

preparation time 20 minutes **serves** 4
nutritional count per serving 3.5g total fat (0.6g saturated fat); 790kJ (189 cal); 19.4g carbohydrate; 18g protein; 3g fibre
tips you can use an equal weight of prawns or lobster instead of the crab meat in this salad.
Make sure your mango is quite firm, otherwise it will not slice well.

Chilli squid salad

3 cleaned squid hoods (450g)
1 tablespoon sweet chilli sauce
2 teaspoons fish sauce
2 teaspoons lime juice
1 tablespoon peanut oil
1 telegraph cucumber (400g), halved lengthways, sliced thinly
3 green onions, sliced thinly
1 cup (80g) bean sprouts
¼ cup firmly packed fresh coriander leaves
⅓ cup firmly packed fresh mint leaves
1 fresh long red chilli, sliced thinly
¼ cup (60ml) sweet chilli sauce, extra
1 tablespoon lime juice, extra

1 Cut squid hoods in half lengthways; score inside in diagonal pattern. Cut each half in four pieces.
2 Combine squid, sauces and juice in medium bowl.
3 Heat oil in wok; stir-fry squid, in batches, until cooked through.
4 Place squid in large bowl with remaining ingredients; toss gently to combine.

preparation time 15 minutes **cooking time** 10 minutes **serves** 4
nutritional count per serving 6.6g total fat (1.4g saturated fat); 744kJ (178 cal); 6.5g carbohydrate; 21.4g protein; 3g fibre

Ruby red grapefruit, smoked salmon and mizuna salad

300g sliced smoked salmon
2 ruby red grapefruits (700g)
2 tablespoons olive oil
1 teaspoon dijon mustard
150g mizuna
⅓ cup (50g) roasted cashews, chopped coarsely
½ small red onion (50g), sliced thinly

1 Reserve four slices of salmon; cut remaining slices into thick pieces.
2 Segment grapefruits over large bowl. Add oil, mustard, mizuna, nuts, onion and salmon pieces; toss gently to combine.
3 Divide salad among serving plates; top with reserved salmon slices.

preparation time 15 minutes **serves** 4
nutritional count per serving 19.1g total fat (3g saturated fat); 1229kJ (294 cal); 8.6g carbohydrate; 21.1g protein; 2.4g fibre

Chorizo, curly endive, orange and walnut salad

2 chorizo sausages (340g), sliced thinly
2 medium oranges (480g)
150g curly endive, trimmed
¾ cup (75g) roasted walnuts
walnut orange dressing
¼ cup (60ml) walnut oil
1 teaspoon finely grated orange rind
¼ cup (60ml) orange juice
1 teaspoon dijon mustard

1 Cook chorizo in large frying pan, stirring occasionally, until browned. Cool 10 minutes.
2 Meanwhile, make walnut orange dressing.
3 Segment oranges over large bowl. Add chorizo, endive, nuts and dressing; toss gently to combine.
walnut orange dressing place ingredients in screw-top jar; shake well.

preparation time 10 minutes **cooking time** 5 minutes **serves** 4
nutritional count per serving 52.3g total fat (12.6g saturated fat); 2500kJ (598 cal); 10.9g carbohydrate; 20.7g protein; 4.2g fibre

Shaved fennel and apple salad with brie and pecans

2 baby fennel (260g)
2 medium green apples (300g)
1 cup (120g) roasted pecans
1 red coral lettuce, trimmed, chopped coarsely
150g brie cheese, sliced
mustard vinaigrette
⅓ cup (80ml) olive oil
¼ cup (60ml) lemon juice
1 tablespoon wholegrain mustard

1 Make mustard vinaigrette.
2 Trim and halve fennel; reserve 2 tablespoons coarsely chopped frond tips. Halve and core unpeeled apples. Using a very sharp knife, mandoline or V-slicer, slice fennel and apple thinly.
3 Place fennel and apple in large bowl with frond tips, nuts and dressing; toss gently to combine. Serve salad on top of lettuce, top with cheese.
mustard vinaigrette place ingredients in screw-top jar; shake well.

preparation time 20 minutes **serves** 6
nutritional count per serving 33.3g total fat (6.8g saturated fat); 1496kJ (358 cal); 6.6g carbohydrate; 7.4g protein; 3.5g fibre
tip we used a brie cheese here. It can be replaced with its blue-vein counterpart, if you prefer, but select one that's mild and very creamy.

Swiss brown mushroom and warm pancetta salad

200g swiss brown mushrooms, quartered
¼ cup (60ml) balsamic vinegar
8 slices pancetta (120g)
100g baby spinach leaves, trimmed
2 tablespoons drained baby capers, rinsed
2 green onions, chopped finely
1 tablespoon olive oil
1 clove garlic, crushed

1 Combine mushrooms with 2 tablespoons of the vinegar in small bowl.
2 Cook pancetta in medium oiled frying pan until crisp; chop coarsely.
3 Drain mushrooms; discard vinegar. Cook mushrooms in same pan until tender.
4 Place mushrooms and pancetta in large bowl with remaining ingredients and remaining vinegar; toss gently to combine.

preparation time 10 minutes **cooking time** 10 minutes **serves** 6
nutritional count per serving 6g total fat (1.5g saturated fat); 360kJ (86 cal); 1.3g carbohydrate; 5.6g protein; 1.6g fibre

Smoked chicken chow-mein salad with raspberry macadamia dressing

100g packet fried noodles
½ cup (70g) roasted macadamias, chopped coarsely
100g baby rocket leaves
100g mizuna
1 small red onion (100g), sliced thinly
½ cup firmly packed fresh flat-leaf parsley leaves
½ cup firmly packed fresh mint leaves
800g smoked chicken breast fillets, sliced thinly
raspberry macadamia dressing
2 cloves garlic, crushed
¼ cup (60ml) raspberry vinegar
1 tablespoon wholegrain mustard
⅓ cup (80ml) macadamia oil

1 Make raspberry macadamia dressing.
2 Place salad ingredients in large bowl with dressing; toss gently
to combine.
raspberry macadamia dressing place ingredients in screw-top jar;
shake well.

preparation time 20 minutes **serves** 6
nutritional count per serving 32.3g total fat (6.3g saturated fat);
1923kJ (460 cal); 5.8g carbohydrate; 35.5g protein; 2.8g fibre

Barbecued pork and crunchy noodle salad

10 trimmed red radishes (150g), sliced thinly, cut into matchsticks
1 large red capsicum (350g) sliced thinly
2 baby buk choy (300g), sliced thinly
6 green onions, sliced thinly
1 cup (80g) bean sprouts
½ cup (70g) roasted slivered almonds
2 x 100g packets fried noodles
400g chinese barbecued pork, sliced thinly
sweet-sour dressing
¼ cup (60ml) peanut oil
2 tablespoons white vinegar
2 tablespoons brown sugar
2 tablespoons light soy sauce
1 teaspoon sesame oil
1 clove garlic, crushed

1 Make sweet-sour dressing.
2 Place salad ingredients in large bowl with dressing; toss gently to combine.
sweet-sour dressing place ingredients in screw-top jar; shake well.

preparation time 20 minutes **serves** 6
nutritional count per serving 29.7g total fat (7.6g saturated fat);
1789kJ (428 cal); 17.6g carbohydrate; 20.4g protein; 6.1g fibre

Turkish haloumi and pomegranate salad

1 tablespoon lemon juice
2 tablespoons light olive oil
⅓ cup (80ml) pomegranate pulp
¼ cup firmly packed fresh mint leaves
2 green onions, sliced thinly
125g mizuna
1 medium fennel (300g), trimmed, sliced thinly
360g haloumi cheese, sliced thickly

1 Place juice, oil, pomegranate, mint, onion, mizuna and fennel in large bowl; toss gently to combine.
2 Cook cheese in large oiled frying pan until brown both sides.
3 Serve salad topped with cheese.

preparation time 15 minutes **cooking time** 5 minutes **serves** 4
nutritional count per serving 24.7g total fat (11.2g saturated fat); 1400kJ (335 cal); 6.5g carbohydrate; 20.6g protein; 3.5g fibre

Black-eyed beans, tomato and rocket salad

1 cup (200g) dried black-eyed beans
175g baby green beans, trimmed, chopped coarsely
1 medium red onion (170g), sliced thinly
250g cherry tomatoes, halved
250g yellow teardrop tomatoes, halved
100g baby rocket leaves
lemon and basil dressing
¼ cup (60ml) lemon juice
1 tablespoon olive oil
1 tablespoon dijon mustard
1 clove garlic, crushed
1 tablespoon finely chopped fresh basil

1 Cook black-eyed beans in medium saucepan of boiling water, about 30 minutes or until just tender; drain. Rinse under cold water; drain.
2 Meanwhile, boil, steam or microwave green beans until just tender; drain. Rinse under cold water; drain.
3 Make lemon and basil dressing.
4 Place black-eyed beans and green beans in large bowl with remaining ingredients and dressing; toss gently to combine.
lemon and basil dressing place ingredients in screw-top jar; shake well.

preparation time 20 minutes **cooking time** 30 minutes **serves** 4
nutritional count per serving 6.1g total fat (0.8g saturated fat); 915kJ (219 cal); 26.3g carbohydrate; 15.3g protein; 11.2g fibre

Salad of grilled vegetables, haloumi and rosemary chicken

2 tablespoons olive oil
1 tablespoon balsamic vinegar
2 cloves garlic, crushed
1 tablespoon coarsely chopped fresh rosemary
800g chicken thigh fillets
600g piece pumpkin, trimmed, sliced thinly
300g asparagus, trimmed
2 x 180g packets haloumi cheese, thickly sliced
250g baby rocket leaves
rosemary balsamic dressing
2 tablespoons olive oil
1 tablespoon balsamic vinegar
1 tablespoon lemon juice
1 tablespoon coarsely chopped fresh rosemary leaves

1 Make rosemary balsamic dressing.
2 Combine oil, vinegar, garlic, rosemary and chicken in medium bowl.
3 Cook chicken mixture on heated oiled grill plate (or grill or barbecue); cover chicken.
4 Cook pumpkin and asparagus, in batches, on grill plate until tender. Transfer to large bowl; cover.
5 Cook cheese on cleaned grill plate until brown both sides.
6 Slice chicken thickly, add to pumpkin and asparagus along with cheese, rocket and dressing; toss gently to combine.
rosemary balsamic dressing place ingredients in screw-top jar; shake well.

preparation time 15 minutes **cooking time** 35 minutes **serves** 4
nutritional count per serving 49.1g total fat (17.2g saturated fat);
3106kJ (743 cal); 12.2g carbohydrate; 62.6g protein; 3.8g fibre

Mixed vegetable salad with peanut sauce

4 medium carrots (480g), cut into batons
1 medium potato (200g), chopped coarsely
200g cauliflower, cut into florets
100g snow peas, trimmed, halved
1 lebanese cucumber (130g), cut into batons
1½ cups (100g) coarsely chopped iceberg lettuce
1½ cups (120g) bean sprouts
½ cup coarsely chopped fresh coriander
peanut sauce
½ cup (70g) toasted unsalted peanuts
2 cloves garlic, quartered
4 green onions, chopped coarsely
½ teaspoon brown sugar
1 tablespoon soy sauce
½ teaspoon chilli powder
1 tablespoon lemon juice
¾ cup (180ml) water
140ml can light coconut milk

1 Boil, steam or microwave carrot, potato, cauliflower and peas,
separately, until just tender; drain. Rinse under cold water; drain.
2 Meanwhile, make peanut sauce.
3 Place cooked vegetables in large bowl with cucumber, lettuce,
sprouts and coriander; toss gently to combine.
4 Serve salad drizzled with peanut sauce.
peanut sauce using mortar and pestle, grind nuts until crushed finely;
transfer to small bowl. Using mortar and pestle, crush garlic and green
onion into a coarse paste. Cook garlic mixture in medium oiled frying
pan, stirring, 2 minutes. Add remaining ingredients; bring to the boil.
Reduce heat; simmer, uncovered, 3 minutes. Add nuts; simmer,
uncovered, 5 minutes.

preparation time 30 minutes **cooking time** 15 minutes **serves** 4
nutritional count per serving 9.8g total fat (8.8g saturated fat);
1208kJ (289 cal); 20.3g carbohydrate; 11.1g protein; 9.2g fibre

Egg, potato and spinach salad

8 kipfler or tiny new potatoes
6 eggs
4 rashers rindless bacon (260g), sliced thickly
100g baby spinach leaves
¼ cup coarsely chopped fresh chives
60g parmesan cheese, shaved
mustard dressing
2 tablespoons olive oil
1 tablespoon red wine vinegar
2 teaspoons wholegrain mustard

1 Boil, steam or microwave potatoes until tender; drain. Slice potatoes thickly.
2 Place eggs in small saucepan, cover with cold water. Bring to the boil, stirring (this will centre the yolks), then simmer, uncovered, 5 minutes. Drain, cover with cold water, then remove the shells. Quarter eggs lengthways.
3 Cook bacon in large frying pan until crisp; drain on absorbent paper.
4 Make mustard dressing.
5 Place potato and bacon in large bowl with spinach, chives and dressing; toss gently to combine.
6 Divide salad among serving plates, add egg and parmesan flakes.
mustard dressing place ingredients in screw-top jar; shake well.

preparation time 20 minutes **cooking time** 20 minutes **serves** 4
nutritional count per serving 24.5g total fat (7.7g saturated fat); 1488kJ (356 cal); 11.1g carbohydrate; 22g protein; 2.4g fibre

Cos, avocado and tomato salad

1 baby cos lettuce
3 medium tomatoes (450g), chopped finely
2 medium avocados (500g), chopped finely
1 lebanese cucumber (130g), chopped finely
1 small red onion (100g), chopped finely
¼ cup coarsely chopped fresh coriander
¼ cup (60ml) lime juice
2 cloves garlic, crushed

1 Separate lettuce leaves. Reserve several of the larger leaves; shred remaining leaves coarsely.
2 Place shredded lettuce in medium bowl with remaining ingredients; toss gently to combine.
3 Serve salad divided among reserved leaves.

preparation time 15 minutes **serves** 4
nutritional count per serving 20.2g total fat (4.3g saturated fat); 970kJ (232 cal); 5.8g carbohydrate; 4.3g protein; 4.8g fibre

Warm pasta, pea and ricotta salad

375g orecchiette pasta
1½ cups (200g) frozen baby peas
½ cup coarsely chopped fresh mint
100g shaved ham, chopped coarsely
1 teaspoon finely grated lemon rind
200g ricotta cheese, crumbled
buttermilk aïoli
⅓ cup (100g) mayonnaise
2 tablespoons buttermilk
2 teaspoons lemon juice
1 clove garlic, crushed
1 teaspoon finely grated lemon rind

1 Cook pasta in large saucepan of boiling water until just tender; drain.
2 Boil, steam or microwave peas until tender; drain.
3 Meanwhile, make buttermilk aïoli.
4 Place warm pasta and peas in large bowl with mint, ham, rind and aïoli; toss gently to combine. Serve salad sprinkled with cheese.
buttermilk aïoli combine ingredients in small bowl.

preparation time 10 minutes **cooking time** 15 minutes **serves** 4
nutritional count per serving 16.2g total fat (5.2g saturated fat); 2328kJ (557 cal); 74.5g carbohydrate; 24.3g protein; 6.8g fibre
tip if you can't find orecchiette pasta, replace it with penne, the quill-shaped pasta.

Chermoulla chicken with chickpea salad

1 cup (200g) dried chickpeas
4 single chicken breast fillets (680g)
1 medium red capsicum (150g), chopped finely
1 medium green capsicum (150g), chopped finely
2 large egg tomatoes (180g), chopped finely
1 small white onion (80g), chopped finely
2 tablespoons lemon juice
chermoulla
½ cup finely chopped fresh coriander
½ cup finely chopped fresh flat-leaf parsley
3 cloves garlic, crushed
2 tablespoons white wine vinegar
2 tablespoons lemon juice
1 teaspoon sweet paprika
½ teaspoon ground cumin
2 tablespoons olive oil

1 Place chickpeas in large bowl of cold water; stand overnight, drain. Rinse under cold water; drain. Cook chickpeas in medium saucepan of boiling water until just tender; drain. Rinse under cold water; drain.
2 Meanwhile, combine ingredients for chermoulla in large bowl; reserve half of the chermoulla for chickpea salad.
3 Add chicken to large bowl; toss to coat in chermoulla. Cook chicken, in batches, on heated oiled grill plate (or grill or barbecue) until cooked through. Cover to keep warm.
4 Place chickpeas in large bowl with capsicums, tomato, onion and reserved chermoulla; toss gently to combine.
5 Serve chickpea salad with sliced chicken, drizzled with juice.

preparation time 25 minutes (plus standing time)
cooking time 20 minutes **serves** 4
nutritional count per serving 21.6g total fat (4.6g saturated fat); 1994kJ (477 cal); 22.5g carbohydrate; 47.2g protein; 9g fibre
tip chermoulla is a Moroccan blend of fresh and ground herbs and spices, including cumin, coriander and paprika, traditionally used for preserving or seasoning meat, poultry or fish. We used it as a quick flavouring for both the chicken and salad, to bring both elements of this recipe together.

Crisp-fried duck with mango and chilli-lime green salad

You need to buy a large chinese barbecued duck and a small bunch of silver beet for this recipe.

¼ cup (60ml) lime juice
1 tablespoon sweet chilli sauce
1kg chinese barbecued duck
2 teaspoons peanut oil
500g silver beet, trimmed, chopped coarsely
1 cup loosely packed fresh coriander leaves
3 cups (240g) bean sprouts
1 medium mango (430g), sliced thinly
2 limes, cut into wedges

1 Combine juice and sauce in small jug.
2 Remove skin then meat from duck; discard bones, slice skin thinly.
3 Heat oil in wok; stir-fry skin until crisp. Drain. Slice duck meat thinly; stir-fry until hot.
4 Combine silver beet, coriander, sprouts, mango, duck and juice mixture in large bowl; toss gently to combine. Sprinkle salad with slivered duck skin, serve with lime wedges.

preparation time 20 minutes **cooking time** 10 minutes **serves** 4
nutritional count per serving 39.8g total fat (11.6g saturated fat); 2261kJ (541 cal); 12.5g carbohydrate; 31.8g protein; 4.7g fibre

Asian millet and tofu salad

1 cup (200g) millet
2 fresh long red chillies, chopped finely
⅓ cup (45g) roasted unsalted coarsely chopped peanuts
400g firm marinated tofu, cut into matchsticks
100g snow peas, trimmed, sliced lengthways
230g can bamboo shoots, rinsed, drained, sliced thinly
½ small red onion (50g), sliced thinly
mirin dressing
¼ cup (60ml) mirin
1 tablespoon japanese soy sauce
1 tablespoon rice vinegar
1 clove garlic, crushed

1 Cook millet in medium saucepan of boiling water until just tender;
drain. Cool.
2 Meanwhile, make mirin dressing.
3 Place millet in large bowl with chilli, nuts and half of the dressing;
toss gently to combine.
4 Place tofu and remaining ingredients in medium bowl with remaining
dressing; toss gently to combine.
5 Serve millet mixture topped with tofu salad.
mirin dressing place ingredients in screw-top jar; shake well.

preparation time 20 minutes
cooking time 15 minutes (plus cooling time) **serves** 4
nutritional count per serving 14.4g total fat (2.2g saturated fat);
1676kJ (401 cal); 39.3g carbohydrate; 22g protein; 8.8g fibre
tip we used cryovac-packed ready-to-serve sweet chilli tofu, available
from many supermarkets and Asian food stores.

Tuna and cannellini bean salad

2 cups (400g) dried cannellini beans
425g can tuna in springwater, drained
1 small red onion (100g), sliced thinly
2 trimmed celery stalks (200g), sliced thinly
italian dressing
⅓ cup (80ml) olive oil
⅓ cup (80ml) lemon juice
1 tablespoon finely chopped fresh oregano
2 cloves garlic, crushed

1 Place beans in medium bowl, cover with cold water; stand overnight,
drain. Rinse under cold water; drain. Place beans in medium saucepan of
boiling water; return to the boil. Reduce heat; simmer, uncovered, about
1 hour or until beans are almost tender. Drain.
2 Meanwhile, make italian dressing.
3 Combine beans and dressing in large bowl with tuna, onion and celery.
italian dressing place ingredients in screw-top jar; shake well.

preparation time 10 minutes (plus standing time)
cooking time 1 hour **serves** 4
nutritional count per serving 21.6g total fat (3.8g saturated fat);
1651kJ (395 cal); 17.3g carbohydrate; 28.8g protein; 8.5g fibre

Coconut-poached chicken with thai-flavours salad

2 x 400ml cans coconut milk
1 tablespoon coarsely chopped fresh coriander root and stem mixture
2 cloves garlic, sliced thinly
2 fresh kaffir lime leaves, shredded finely
800g chicken breast fillets
10cm stick fresh lemon grass (20g)
1 lebanese cucumber (130g), halved lengthways, seeded, sliced thinly
1½ cups (120g) bean sprouts
¾ cup loosely packed fresh coriander leaves
½ cup loosely packed fresh mint leaves
1 fresh long red chilli, sliced thinly
coriander and lime dressing
2 teaspoons coarsely chopped fresh coriander root and stem mixture
2 cloves garlic, peeled
2 fresh small red thai chillies
1 tablespoon caster sugar
¼ cup (60ml) lime juice
2 teaspoons fish sauce

1 Bring coconut milk, coriander mixture, garlic and lime leaves to the boil in large saucepan. Add chicken; return to the boil. Reduce heat; simmer, uncovered, about 10 minutes or until cooked through. Remove from heat; stand chicken in poaching liquid 10 minutes. Remove chicken from pan; when cool enough to handle, shred coarsely.
2 Reserve 1 cup poaching liquid; discard remainder. Bring reserved liquid to the boil in same pan; boil, uncovered, about 10 minutes or until reduced by two-thirds. Add chicken to pan with liquid; cool 10 minutes.
3 Meanwhile, make coriander and lime dressing.
4 Soak lemon grass in boiling water about 4 minutes or until just tender; drain. Slice thinly; combine in large bowl with cucumber, sprouts, herbs, chilli and dressing. Divide chicken among serving plates; top with salad.
coriander and lime dressing using mortar and pestle, crush coriander mixture, garlic, chillies and sugar until combined. Gradually add juice; crush until sugar dissolves. Stir in fish sauce.
preparation time 30 minutes **cooking time** 25 minutes **serves** 4
nutritional count per serving 52.7g total fat (39.7g saturated fat); 3056kJ (731 cal); 13.9g carbohydrate; 48.7g protein; 6g fibre

Smoked trout and potato salad

750g baby new potatoes, halved
2 x 385g whole smoked trout
1 small red onion (100g), sliced thinly
2 green onions, sliced thinly
2 tablespoons drained capers, rinsed
1 tablespoon finely chopped fresh dill
4 large iceberg lettuce leaves
dressing
2 tablespoons lemon juice
1 tablespoon olive oil
1 teaspoon dijon mustard

1 Boil, steam or microwave potato until tender; drain. Cook potato on heated oiled grill plate (or grill or barbecue) until browned both sides.
2 Meanwhile, discard skin and bones from fish; flake flesh into large bowl.
3 Make dressing.
4 Add potato to large bowl along with onions, capers and dill; toss gently to combine. Divide salad among lettuce leaves.
dressing place ingredients in screw-top jar; shake well.

preparation time 5 minutes **cooking time** 25 minutes **serves** 4
nutritional count per serving 16.6g total fat (1.9g saturated fat); 1404kJ (336 cal); 27.6g carbohydrate; 31.2g protein; 4.8g fibre

Warm lentil and chorizo salad

1 ¼ cups (250g) french green lentils
1 small brown onion (80g), quartered
1 bay leaf
2 chorizo sausages (340g), sliced thinly
3 shallots (75g), sliced thinly
2 trimmed celery stalks (200g), sliced diagonally
1 cup coarsely chopped fresh flat-leaf parsley
macadamia dressing
½ cup (125ml) red wine vinegar
⅓ cup (80ml) macadamia oil

1 Cook lentils, onion and bay leaf in large saucepan of boiling water, uncovered, about 15 minutes or until lentils are tender; drain. Discard onion and bay leaf.
2 Cook chorizo in large frying pan, stirring occasionally, until browned. Drain; cool 10 minutes.
3 Make macadamia dressing.
4 Place lentils and chorizo in large bowl with shallot, celery, parsley and dressing; toss gently to combine.
macadamia dressing place ingredients in screw-top jar; shake well.

preparation time 15 minutes **cooking time** 25 minutes **serves** 6
nutritional count per serving 30.2g total fat (8.1g saturated fat);
1860kJ (445 cal); 19.1g carbohydrate; 21.8g protein; 7.3g fibre

Prawn and vermicelli salad

60g rice vermicelli noodles
400g cooked medium king prawns
2 green onions, sliced thinly
1 small red capsicum (150g), sliced thinly
1 small green capsicum (150g), sliced thinly
1 lebanese cucumber (130g), seeded, sliced thinly
2 tablespoons finely shredded fresh vietnamese mint
¼ cup loosely packed fresh coriander leaves
1 tablespoon fried shallots
dressing
1½ tablespoons fish sauce
1 tablespoon lime juice
1 tablespoon water
2 teaspoons brown sugar

1 Place vermicelli in large heatproof bowl, cover with boiling water;
stand until just tender, drain. Cut into random lengths.
2 Make dressing.
3 Shell and devein prawns; halve prawns lengthways.
4 Place vermicelli and prawns in large serving bowl with onion,
capsicums, cucumber, herbs and dressing; toss gently to combine.
Top with shallots; serve immediately.
dressing place ingredients in screw-top jar; shake well.

preparation time 20 minutes **cooking time** 5 minutes **serves** 4
nutritional count per serving 0.7g total fat (0.1g saturated fat);
477kJ (114 cal); 12.9g carbohydrate; 12.9g protein; 1.4g fibre

Pork salad with chilli plum dressing

1 medium wombok (1kg), shredded finely
½ cup finely shredded fresh mint
1 small red onion (100g), sliced thinly
400g leftover roast pork, shredded finely
½ cup firmly packed fresh mint leaves
chilli plum dressing
½ cup (150g) mayonnaise
½ cup (125ml) plum sauce
1 teaspoon dried chilli flakes
2 tablespoons water

1 Make chilli plum dressing.
2 Place wombok, shredded mint, onion, half the pork and half the dressing in large bowl; toss gently to combine.
3 Divide wombok mixture among serving plates; top with remaining pork and mint leaves, drizzle with remaining dressing.
chilli plum dressing whisk ingredients in small bowl.

preparation time 20 minutes **serves** 4
nutritional count per serving 16.6g total fat (4g saturated fat); 1889kJ (452 cal); 31.7g carbohydrate; 32.8g protein; 8.9g fibre

Turkish lamb and yogurt salad

600g lamb backstrap
2 tablespoons sumac
1 tablespoon olive oil
250g cherry tomatoes, halved
2 lebanese cucumbers (260g), seeded, sliced thinly
½ cup loosely packed fresh flat-leaf parsley leaves
½ cup loosely packed fresh mint leaves
1 small red onion (100g), sliced thinly
yogurt dressing
¼ cup (70g) yogurt
2 tablespoons lemon juice

1 Rub lamb with sumac. Heat oil in large frying pan; cook lamb until cooked as desired. Cover, stand 5 minutes; slice thinly.
2 Meanwhile, make yogurt dressing.
3 Place lamb and remaining ingredients in large bowl with dressing; toss gently to combine.
yogurt dressing whisk ingredients in small jug.

preparation time 15 minutes **cooking time** 10 minutes **serves** 4
nutritional count per serving 10.8g total fat (3.4g saturated fat);
1062kJ (254 cal); 5.1g carbohydrate; 32.9g protein; 2.7g fibre
tip sumac is a purple-red, astringent spice ground from berries growing on shrubs that flourish wild around the Mediterranean. It adds a tart, lemony flavour to dips and dressings and goes well with barbecued meat. Can be found in Middle Eastern food stores.

Smoked chicken and cranberry salad

500g smoked chicken breast fillets, sliced thinly
1 large green apple (200g), sliced thinly
1 cup (120g) roasted pecans
½ cup (65g) dried cranberries
150g baby spinach leaves
1 cup loosely packed fresh parsley leaves
dressing
2 teaspoons dijon mustard
¼ cup (60ml) apple cider vinegar
2 tablespoons olive oil

1 Make dressing.
2 Place chicken in large bowl with remaining salad ingredients and dressing; toss gently to combine.
dressing place ingredients in screw-top jar; shake well.

preparation time 15 minutes **serves** 4
nutritional count per serving 39.8g total fat (5.2g saturated fat); 2420kJ (579 cal); 17.7g carbohydrate; 35.5g protein; 5.9g fibre

Beetroot and lentil salad with grilled pork sausages

1 ½ cups (350g) french green lentils
2 sprigs fresh thyme
850g small beetroots, trimmed
1 tablespoon olive oil
1 large brown onion (200g), chopped finely
2 teaspoons yellow mustard seeds
2 teaspoons ground cumin
1 teaspoon ground coriander
½ cup (125ml) chicken stock
150g baby spinach leaves
8 thick pork sausages (960g)
thyme dressing
1 teaspoon fresh thyme
1 clove garlic, crushed
½ cup (125ml) red wine vinegar
¼ cup (60ml) olive oil

1 Make thyme dressing.
2 Cook lentils and thyme in large saucepan of boiling water until lentils are just tender; drain, discard thyme. Place lentils in large bowl with half of the dressing; toss gently to combine.
3 Meanwhile, discard any leaves and all but 2cm of the stalk from each beetroot. Boil, steam or microwave unpeeled beetroots until just tender; drain. When cool enough to handle, peel then quarter beetroots; add to lentils.
4 Heat oil in large frying pan; cook onion, seeds and spices, stirring, until onion softens. Add stock; bring to the boil. Remove from heat; stir in spinach.
5 Add spinach mixture and remaining dressing to lentil and beetroot mixture; toss gently to combine.
6 Cook sausages in same cleaned pan until cooked through; serve sliced sausages with beetroot and lentil salad.
thyme dressing place ingredients in screw-top jar; shake well.

preparation time 25 minutes **cooking time** 50 minutes **serves** 4
nutritional count per serving 73.7g total fat (24.5g saturated fat); 4623kJ (1106 cal); 58.7g carbohydrate; 55.5g protein; 22.6g fibre

Avocado caesar salad

2 small white bread rolls (80g), sliced thinly
1 clove garlic, crushed
1 tablespoon olive oil
2 baby cos lettuce
1 medium red onion (170g), sliced thinly
2 medium avocados (500g), chopped coarsely
⅓ cup (50g) sun-dried tomatoes in oil, drained, sliced thinly
60g parmesan cheese, shaved
dressing
1 clove garlic, crushed
2 egg yolks
2 teaspoons dijon mustard
2 tablespoons white vinegar
¾ cup (180ml) extra light olive oil
1 tablespoon water, approximately

1 Preheat oven to 200°C/180°C fan-forced.
2 Place bread slices, in single layer, on oven tray; brush with combined garlic and oil. Toast in oven about 5 minutes or until crisp.
3 Meanwhile, make dressing.
4 Place toast in large bowl with remaining ingredients and dressing; toss gently to combine.
dressing blend or process garlic, yolks, mustard and vinegar until smooth. With motor operating, gradually add oil in a thin steady stream; process until mixture thickens. Add enough water, if desired, to make pouring consistency.

preparation time 20 minutes **cooking time** 5 minutes **serves** 4
nutritional count per serving 75.1g total fat (14.9g saturated fat); 3394kJ (812 cal); 19.4g carbohydrate; 14.1g protein; 6.6g fibre
tip garlic toasts can be made a day ahead; store in an airtight container.

Asian duck salad

1kg chinese barbecued duck
150g snow peas, trimmed, sliced thinly
1 green mango (350g), sliced thinly
3 shallots (75g), sliced thinly
125g mizuna
⅓ cup firmly packed fresh mint leaves
⅓ cup firmly packed fresh coriander leaves
1 fresh long red chilli, sliced thinly
thai dressing
2 tablespoons fish sauce
2 tablespoons grated palm sugar
⅓ cup (80ml) lime juice
2 teaspoons peanut oil

1 Make thai dressing.
2 Remove meat, leaving skin on, from duck; discard bones. Chop duck meat coarsely.
3 Place duck in large bowl with remaining ingredients and dressing; toss gently to combine.
thai dressing place ingredients in screw-top jar; shake well.

preparation time 25 minutes **serves** 4
nutritional count per serving 39.8g total fat (11.5g saturated fat); 2337kJ (559 cal); 17.8g carbohydrate; 31.7g protein; 3.2g fibre

Turkey, cranberry and peanut salad in butter lettuce leaves

1.5kg boneless turkey breast
1.5 litres (6 cups) water
½ cup (125ml) red wine vinegar
1 teaspoon dijon mustard
¼ cup (60ml) light olive oil
⅔ cup (90g) dried cranberries
3 trimmed celery stalks (300g), sliced thinly
1¼ cups (100g) bean sprouts
1 cup (50g) snow pea sprouts
½ cup (70g) roasted unsalted peanuts
½ cup firmly packed fresh mint leaves, torn
1 butter lettuce, leaves separated

1 Cut turkey into three equal-sized pieces. Bring the water to the boil in large saucepan; add turkey. Simmer, covered, about 35 minutes or until turkey is cooked. Cool turkey in poaching liquid 15 minutes. Drain turkey; shred coarsely.
2 Combine vinegar, mustard and oil in large bowl. Add turkey, cranberries, celery, sprouts, nuts and mint; toss gently to combine.
3 Serve salad with lettuce leaves.

preparation time 30 minutes (plus cooling time)
cooking time 40 minutes **serves** 6
nutritional count per serving 23.1g total fat (4.1g saturated fat);
2019kJ (483 cal); 6.7g carbohydrate; 59.7g protein; 4.2g fibre

Chilli lime chicken salad

2 cups (500ml) water
2 cups (500ml) chicken stock
4 single chicken breasts fillets (680g)
1 small red capsicum (150g), sliced thinly
4 trimmed red radishes (60g), sliced thinly
¼ small wombok (175g), shredded coarsely
3 green onions, sliced thinly
1 cup (80g) bean sprouts
½ cup loosely packed fresh coriander leaves
½ cup (75g) roasted salted peanuts
chilli lime dressing
⅓ cup (80ml) lime juice
¼ cup (65g) grated palm sugar
2 fresh small red thai chillies, chopped finely
1 clove garlic, crushed
1 tablespoon fish sauce
¼ cup (60ml) peanut oil

1 Bring the water and stock to the boil in large frying pan. Add chicken, reduce heat; simmer, covered, about 10 minutes or until cooked through. Remove from heat; cool chicken in poaching liquid 10 minutes. Slice chicken thinly.
2 Meanwhile, make chilli lime dressing.
3 Place remaining salad ingredients in large bowl with half of the dressing; toss gently to combine.
4 Divide salad among serving plates; top with chicken, drizzle with remaining dressing.
chilli lime dressing stir juice, sugar, chilli and garlic in small saucepan over low heat until sugar dissolves; cool 10 minutes. Whisk in sauce and oil.

preparation time 20 minutes **cooking time** 10 minutes **serves** 4
nutritional count per serving 27.2g total fat (4.2g saturated fat);
2157kJ (516 cal); 21.5g carbohydrate; 47g protein; 4g fibre

Vietnamese duck salad

You need one whole chinese barbecued duck for this recipe.

1kg chinese barbecued duck
1 small wombok (700g), shredded finely
1 large carrot (180g), grated coarsely
150g snow peas, sliced thinly lengthways
1 cup (80g) bean sprouts
¼ cup vietnamese mint leaves
lime dressing
½ cup (125ml) lime juice
2 tablespoons fish sauce
2 tablespoons grated palm sugar
2 fresh small red thai chillies, chopped finely

1 Make lime dressing.
2 Remove and discard skin and bones from duck; chop meat coarsely.
3 Place duck in large bowl with remaining salad ingredients and dressing; toss gently to combine.
lime dressing place ingredients in screw-top jar; shake well.

preparation time 30 minutes **serves** 4
nutritional count per serving 38g total fat (11.1g saturated fat); 2270kJ (543 cal); 13.1g carbohydrate; 35.2g protein; 5.3g fibre

Crunchy snow pea, prawn and avocado salad with chive vinaigrette

750g cooked medium king prawns
150g sugar snap peas, trimmed
3 small avocados (600g), sliced thickly
2 cups (100g) snow pea sprouts
chive vinaigrette
¼ cup (60ml) white wine vinegar
¼ cup (60ml) olive oil
¼ cup finely chopped fresh chives

1 Make chive vinaigrette.
2 Shell and devein prawns, leaving tails intact.
3 Boil, steam or microwave peas until just tender; rinse under cold water, drain.
4 Place peas in large bowl with prawns, avocado, sprouts and vinaigrette; toss gently to combine.
chive vinaigrette combine ingredients in small bowl.

preparation time 20 minutes **cooking time** 5 minutes **serves** 4
nutritional count per serving 38.2g total fat (7.2g saturated fat); 1998kJ (478 cal); 8.2g carbohydrate; 24.6g protein; 3.7g fibre

Duck salad with mandarin and pomegranate

You need one large pomegranate for this recipe.

150g sugar snap peas, trimmed
1kg chinese barbecued duck
2 small mandarins (200g), segmented
1 red mignonette lettuce (280g)
⅓ cup (60g) pomegranate pulp
¾ cup (120g) roasted slivered almonds
lemon dijon dressing
1 clove garlic, crushed
1 teaspoon dijon mustard
2 tablespoons lemon juice
2 tablespoons olive oil

1 Boil, steam or microwave peas until just tender; drain. Rinse under cold water; drain.
2 Meanwhile, make lemon dijon dressing.
3 Remove meat, leaving skin on, from duck; discard bones. Chop meat coarsely.
4 Place duck in large bowl with peas, mandarin, lettuce, pomegranate, nuts and dressing; toss gently to combine.
lemon dijon dressing place ingredients in screw-top jar; shake well.

preparation time 25 minutes **cooking time** 5 minutes **serves** 4
nutritional count per serving 58.3g total fat (12.7g saturated fat); 2876kJ (688 cal); 8.9g carbohydrate; 33.3g protein; 6.5g fibre

Black grape, chicken and wild rice salad with tarragon dressing

1 litre (4 cups) water
800g chicken breast fillets
1½ cups (300g) wild rice blend
⅔ cup (110g) roasted blanched almonds
1 cup (190g) black grapes
¼ cup loosely packed fresh tarragon leaves
2 green onions, sliced finely
2 teaspoons finely grated lemon rind
1 tablespoon lemon juice
tarragon dressing
½ cup (120g) sour cream
1 tablespoon dijon mustard
1 tablespoon finely chopped fresh tarragon
1 tablespoon water
2 teaspoons lemon juice

1 Bring the water to the boil in large frying pan; add chicken. Simmer, covered, about 10 minutes or until chicken is cooked. Cool chicken in poaching liquid 10 minutes; drain, slice thickly.
2 Cook rice in large saucepan of boiling water until tender; drain. Cool 10 minutes.
3 Make tarragon dressing.
4 Place rice in large bowl with nuts, grapes, tarragon, onion, rind and juice; toss gently to combine.
5 Serve rice salad topped with chicken, accompanied with dressing.
tarragon dressing combine ingredients in small bowl.

preparation time 20 minutes **cooking time** 25 minutes **serves** 4
nutritional count per serving 32.1g total fat (10g saturated fat); 2575kJ (616 cal); 24.4g carbohydrate; 55.3g protein; 4.5g fibre

Poached salmon and pasta salad with rocket pesto

500g farfalle pasta
800g salmon fillets
1.25 litres (5 cups) water
½ medium lemon (70g), cut into wedges
1 small red onion (100g), sliced thinly
2 tablespoons drained capers, rinsed
2 medium tomatoes (300g), seeded, chopped finely
1 lebanese cucumber (130g), seeded, chopped finely
1 tablespoon finely grated lemon rind
⅓ cup (80ml) lemon juice
rocket pesto
250g rocket, trimmed
¼ cup (20g) coarsely grated parmesan cheese
¼ cup (40g) roasted pine nuts
2 cloves garlic, quartered
½ cup (125ml) olive oil

1 Make rocket pesto.
2 Cook pasta in large saucepan of boiling water until just tender; drain.
3 Halve fish fillets. Bring the water and lemon to the boil in large frying pan. Add fish; simmer, uncovered, until fish is cooked, drain. Cut fish into chunks.
4 Combine pasta, onion, capers, tomato, cucumber, rind and juice in large bowl. Add fish and pesto; toss gently to combine.
rocket pesto Blend or process rocket, cheese, nuts and garlic until smooth. With motor operating, add oil in a thin, steady stream until pesto thickens.

preparation time 25 minutes **cooking time** 25 minutes **serves** 6
nutritional count total fat 35.6g total fat (6g saturated fat);
3089kJ (739 cal); 61.5g carbohydrate; 39.7g protein; 5.4g fibre
tip farfalle is a short, rather sturdy butterfly-shaped pasta that is also known as "bow-ties". It is good for a dish such as this because the folds and crinkles of each piece help capture the pesto and hold the other ingredients. Replace the farfalle with penne or small shells if you wish.

Thai beef salad

¼ cup (60ml) fish sauce
¼ cup (60ml) lime juice
500g beef rump steak
1 tablespoon grated palm sugar
2 teaspoons soy sauce
1 clove garlic, crushed
3 lebanese cucumbers (390g), seeded, sliced thinly
4 fresh small red thai chillies, sliced thinly
4 green onions, sliced thinly
250g cherry tomatoes, halved
¼ cup firmly packed fresh vietnamese mint leaves
½ cup firmly packed fresh coriander leaves
½ cup firmly packed fresh thai basil leaves

1 Combine 2 tablespoons of the fish sauce and 1 tablespoon of the juice in medium bowl with beef. Cover; refrigerate 3 hours or overnight.
2 Drain beef; discard marinade. Cook beef on heated oiled grill plate (or grill or barbecue) until cooked as desired. Cover beef, stand 5 minutes; slice beef thinly.
3 Meanwhile, place sugar, soy sauce, garlic, remaining fish sauce and remaining juice in screw-top jar; shake well.
4 Combine cucumber, chilli, onion, tomato and herbs in large bowl. Add beef and dressing; toss gently to combine.

preparation time 25 minutes (plus refrigeration time)
cooking time 10 minutes **serves** 4
nutritional count per serving 8.7g total fat (3.8g saturated fat); 986kJ (236 cal); 8.2g carbohydrate; 30.6g protein; 3.4g fibre

Char-grilled chilli squid and rice noodle salad

800g cleaned squid hoods
450g fresh wide rice noodles
1 medium red capsicum (200g), sliced thinly
150g snow peas, trimmed, halved
1 lebanese cucumber (130g), seeded, sliced thinly
1 small red onion (100g), sliced thinly
1 cup loosely packed fresh coriander leaves
⅓ cup coarsely chopped fresh mint
sweet chilli dressing
½ cup (125ml) water
⅓ cup (75g) caster sugar
1 tablespoon white vinegar
2 fresh small red thai chillies, chopped finely

1 Cut squid down centre to open out; score the inside in a diagonal pattern. Halve squid lengthways; cut squid into 3cm pieces.
2 Make sweet chilli dressing.
3 Cook squid on heated oiled grill plate (or grill or barbecue), in batches, until tender and browned.
4 Place noodles in large heatproof bowl, cover with boiling water; separate with fork, drain.
5 Place noodles and squid in large serving bowl with remaining salad ingredients and dressing; toss gently to combine.
sweet chilli dressing stir the water and sugar in small saucepan over low heat until sugar dissolves; bring to the boil. Reduce heat; simmer, uncovered, without stirring, about 5 minutes or until syrup thickens slightly. Stir in vinegar and chilli off the heat.

preparation time 15 minutes **cooking time** 15 minutes **serves** 4
nutritional count per serving 3.1g total fat (0.8g saturated fat); 1584kJ (379 cal); 48.3g carbohydrate; 38.1g protein; 2.8g fibre

Pasta salad with green beans and tuna

375g large pasta spirals
250g green beans, trimmed, halved crossways
425g can tuna in oil
1 medium red capsicum (200g), sliced thinly
¾ cup loosely packed fresh flat-leaf parsley leaves
lemon dressing
2 cloves garlic, crushed
1 tablespoon finely grated lemon rind
1 teaspoon cracked black pepper
1 tablespoon lemon juice

1 Cook pasta in large saucepan of boiling water until tender; drain.
Rinse pasta under cold water; drain.
2 Meanwhile, boil, steam or microwave beans until just tender; drain.
Rinse under cold water; drain.
3 Drain tuna over small bowl; reserve oil for dressing. Flake tuna in large
chunks with fork.
4 Make lemon dressing.
5 Place pasta, beans and tuna in large bowl with dressing and remaining
ingredients; toss gently to combine.
lemon dressing place ingredients with reserved oil in screw-top jar;
shake well.

preparation time 10 minutes **cooking time** 10 minutes **serves** 4
nutritional count per serving 26g total fat (3.9g saturated fat);
2750kJ (658 cal); 67.5g carbohydrate; 35g protein; 6.2g fibre

Thai-style green mango salad with seared tuna

1 green mango (350g)
2 teaspoons sesame oil
800g tuna steaks, cut into 3cm pieces
½ teaspoon dried chilli flakes
2 tablespoons toasted sesame seeds
2 cups (100g) snow pea sprouts
½ cup firmly packed fresh coriander leaves
½ cup firmly packed fresh mint leaves
½ small red onion (50g), sliced thinly
lime and ginger dressing
¼ cup (60ml) lime juice
3cm piece fresh ginger (15g), grated
1 tablespoon fish sauce

1 Make lime and ginger dressing.
2 Using vegetable peeler, slice mango into thin ribbons.
3 Combine oil and fish in medium bowl. Cook fish on heated oiled grill plate (or grill or barbecue).
4 Return fish to same cleaned bowl with chilli and seeds; mix gently.
5 Place remaining salad ingredients in another medium bowl with dressing; toss gently to combine. Serve salad topped with fish.
lime and ginger dressing place ingredients in screw-top jar; shake well.

preparation time 20 minutes **cooking time** 10 minutes **serves** 4
nutritional count per serving 17.8g total fat (5.4g saturated fat); 1894kJ (453 cal);15.5g carbohydrate; 55.5g protein; 3.7g fibre

Sesame chicken salad

You need to purchase a large barbecued chicken, weighing about 900g, for this recipe.

150g snow peas
4 cups (400g) shredded cooked chicken
100g snow pea sprouts
2 cups (160g) bean sprouts
2 trimmed celery stalks (200g), sliced thinly
4 green onions, sliced thinly
1 tablespoon toasted sesame seeds
dressing
2 tablespoons peanut oil
2 teaspoons sesame oil
½ teaspoon five-spice powder
2 tablespoons kecap manis
1 tablespoon lime juice

1 Place snow peas in medium bowl. Cover with boiling water; drain immediately. Cover snow peas with cold water in same bowl; stand 2 minutes. Drain; slice thinly.
2 Meanwhile, make dressing.
3 Place snow peas in large bowl with chicken, snow pea sprouts, bean sprouts, celery, onion and dressing; toss gently to combine. Serve salad sprinkled with sesame seeds.
dressing place ingredients in screw-top jar; shake well.

preparation time 15 minutes **serves** 4
nutritional count per serving 16.4g total fat (3.9g saturated fat); 1333kJ (319 cal); 9.8g carbohydrate; 30.8g protein; 4.6g fibre
tip sugar snap peas can also be used in this recipe.

Warm lemon-herbed pasta and fresh salmon salad

1 cup (120g) frozen peas
170g asparagus, trimmed, chopped coarsely
500g piece salmon fillet
625g spinach and ricotta agnolotti pasta
½ cup fresh flat-leaf parsley leaves
1 tablespoon water
¼ cup (60ml) olive oil
1 teaspoon finely grated lemon rind
¼ cup (60ml) lemon juice

1 Boil, steam or microwave peas and asparagus, separately, until just tender; drain. Rinse under cold water; drain.
2 Cook fish on heated oiled grill plate (or grill or barbecue) until browned both sides and cooked as desired. Place fish in large bowl then, using fork, flake into chunks.
3 Meanwhile, cook pasta in large saucepan of boiling water until just tender; drain. Place in bowl with fish.
4 Combine parsley, the water, oil, rind and juice in small jug; pour over fish and pasta. Add peas and asparagus; toss gently to combine.

preparation time 15 minutes **cooking time** 20 minutes **serves** 4
nutritional count per serving 33.7g total fat (10.6g saturated fat); 2428kJ (581 cal); 26.9g carbohydrate; 39.8g protein; 5.5g fibre

Salade niçoise

200g baby green beans, trimmed
2 tablespoons olive oil
1 tablespoon lemon juice
2 tablespoons white wine vinegar
4 medium tomatoes (600g), cut into wedges
4 hard-boiled eggs, quartered
425g can tuna in springwater, drained, flaked
½ cup (80g) drained caperberries, rinsed
½ cup (60g) seeded small black olives
¼ cup firmly packed fresh flat-leaf parsley leaves
440g can drained whole baby new potatoes, rinsed, halved

1 Boil, steam or microwave beans until tender; drain. Rinse under cold water; drain.
2 Whisk oil, juice and vinegar in large bowl, add beans and remaining salad ingredients; toss gently to combine.

preparation time 15 minutes **cooking time** 5 minutes **serves** 4
nutritional count per serving 16.9g total fat (3.7g saturated fat);
1522kJ (364 cal); 19.5g carbohydrate; 30.9g protein; 5.2g fibre
tip instead of the canned tuna, you can char-grill four 200g tuna steaks briefly and centre one of them on each salad serving.

Japanese prawn and soba salad

200g dried soba noodles
10g dried wakame
1 medium carrot (120g)
1 lebanese cucumber (130g)
16 uncooked medium king prawns (720g)
½ sheet toasted nori, shredded finely
miso dressing
1 tablespoon water
2 tablespoons rice vinegar
1 tablespoon yellow miso
1 fresh long red chilli, chopped finely
2cm piece fresh ginger (10g), grated
1 clove garlic, crushed
1 tablespoon peanut oil

1 Cook noodles in medium saucepan of boiling water until just tender;
drain. Rinse noodles under cold water; drain.
2 Place wakame in small bowl, cover with cold water; stand about
10 minutes or until softened. Drain then squeeze out excess water.
Chop coarsely, removing hard ribs or stems.
3 Meanwhile, make miso dressing.
4 Using vegetable peeler, slice carrot and cucumber lengthways into
thin ribbons.
5 Shell and devein prawns, leaving tails intact. Cook prawns in medium
saucepan of boiling water until changed in colour. Drain on absorbent
paper; cool.
6 Place noodles, wakame, carrot, cucumber and prawns in large bowl
with dressing; toss gently to combine. Serve salad sprinkled with nori.
miso dressing place ingredients in screw-top jar; shake well.

preparation time 35 minutes (plus standing time)
cooking time 15 minutes (plus cooling time) **serves** 4
nutritional count per serving 6.1g total fat (1.1g saturated fat);
1329kJ (318 cal); 37.7g carbohydrate; 25.4g protein; 3.9g fibre
tips wakame is a bright-green seaweed. Usually sold dried, it can be
rehydrated by soaking in water for about 10 minutes; discard any hard
stems. Nori is also a type of dried seaweed; sold in thin sheets, plain or
toasted (yaki-nori). Wakame and nori are found in most Asian food shops.

Tamarind, lime and honey chicken salad

¼ cup (60ml) peanut oil
¼ cup (60ml) tamarind concentrate
1 tablespoon honey
2 teaspoons dark soy sauce
½ teaspoon finely grated lime rind
1 tablespoon lime juice
1 clove garlic, crushed
800g chicken breast fillets
½ small wombok (350g), trimmed, shredded finely
4 green onions, sliced thinly
500g red radishes, trimmed, sliced thinly, cut into matchsticks
2 lebanese cucumbers (260g), halved widthways, seeded,
  cut into matchsticks
½ cup loosely packed fresh mint leaves
½ cup loosely packed fresh coriander leaves
⅔ cup (50g) fried shallots
honey lime dressing
1 tablespoon honey
2 tablespoons lime juice
1 teaspoon sesame oil
1 tablespoon dark soy sauce
1 fresh long red chilli, chopped finely

1 Combine 1 tablespoon of the oil, tamarind, honey, sauce, rind, juice and garlic in large bowl with chicken. Cover; refrigerate 3 hours or overnight.
2 Make honey lime dressing.
3 Heat remaining oil in large frying pan; cook chicken mixture, in batches, until cooked through. Stand 5 minutes; slice chicken thickly. Cover to keep warm.
4 Place dressing in large bowl with remaining ingredients; toss gently to combine. Divide salad among plates; top with chicken.
honey lime dressing place ingredients in screw-top jar; shake well.

preparation time 35 minutes (plus refrigeration time)
cooking time 20 minutes **serves** 4
nutritional count per serving 27g total fat (6.1g saturated fat);
2144kJ (513 cal); 19.4g carbohydrate; 46.3g protein; 4.3g fibre

Warm pasta provençale salad

375g rigatoni pasta
600g lamb fillets
¾ cup (115g) seeded black olives, halved
1 cup (150g) drained semi-dried tomatoes in oil, chopped coarsely
400g can artichoke hearts, drained, halved
1 small red onion (100g), sliced thinly
60g baby rocket leaves
½ cup (120g) green olive tapenade
2 tablespoons olive oil
2 tablespoons lemon juice

1 Cook pasta in large saucepan of boiling water until tender; drain.
2 Meanwhile, cook lamb in heated oiled large frying pan until cooked
as desired. Cover; stand 5 minutes, then slice thickly.
3 Place pasta and lamb in large bowl with remaining ingredients;
toss gently to combine. Serve warm.

preparation time 15 minutes **cooking time** 15 minutes **serves** 6
nutritional count per serving 16.9g total fat (3.4g saturated fat);
2203kJ (527 cal); 57.4g carbohydrate; 32g protein; 7.5g fibre
tips rigatoni, a tube-shaped pasta with ridges on the outside, is ideal used
in this salad: its wide hollow centre captures the dish's other ingredients
and the dressing clings to the pasta's indentations.
You can use black olive tapenade in this recipe, if you prefer.

Crab and soba noodle salad with ginger miso dressing

270g soba noodles
1 lebanese cucumber (130g), seeded, sliced thinly
1 small red onion (100g), chopped finely
1 medium carrot (120g), cut into matchsticks
50g baby spinach leaves, sliced thinly
400g fresh crab meat
1 tablespoon drained pickled ginger, sliced thinly
ginger miso dressing
6cm piece fresh ginger (30g), chopped coarsely
2 tablespoons drained pickled ginger
2 cloves garlic
⅓ cup (100g) yellow miso paste
½ teaspoon wasabi paste
½ cup (125ml) rice vinegar
½ cup (125ml) vegetable oil
2 tablespoons water

1 Make ginger miso dressing.
2 Cook noodles in large saucepan of boiling water until just tender; drain. Rinse under cold water; drain.
3 Place noodles in large bowl with cucumber, onion, carrot, spinach, half the crab and half the dressing; toss gently to combine.
4 Divide salad among serving plates; top with remaining crab, ginger and remaining dressing.
ginger miso dressing blend or process ingredients until smooth.

preparation time 10 minutes   **cooking time** 20 minutes   **serves** 4
nutritional count per serving 32.4g total fat (4g saturated fat);
2805kJ (671 cal); 55.9g carbohydrate; 35.9g protein; 5.9g fibre

Cajun-spiced beef and garlicky bean salad

750g piece beef fillet
1 tablespoon cajun spice mix
420g can mixed beans, rinsed, drained
2 lebanese cucumbers (260g), halved lengthways, sliced thinly
4 small tomatoes (360g), cut into wedges
1 medium red onion (170g), sliced thinly
1 medium avocado (250g), sliced thickly
½ cup finely chopped fresh coriander
garlic vinaigrette
¼ cup (60ml) lemon juice
¼ cup (60ml) olive oil
2 cloves garlic, crushed

1 Sprinkle beef both sides with spice mix; cook on heated oiled grill plate (or grill or barbecue). Cover; stand 5 minutes then slice thinly.
2 Meanwhile, make garlic vinaigrette.
3 Place remaining salad ingredients in large bowl with vinaigrette; toss gently to combine. Serve salad topped with beef.
garlic vinaigrette combine ingredients in small bowl.

preparation time 15 minutes **cooking time** 10 minutes **serves** 4
nutritional count per serving 35.3g total fat (8.8g saturated fat);
2445kJ (585 cal); 16.3g carbohydrate; 47.5g protein; 7.5 g fibre
tip cajun spice mix, a blend of ground herbs and spices that can include basil, paprika, tarragon, fennel, thyme or cayenne, is available at most supermarkets and specialty spice shops.

Chicken caesar salad

4 slices white bread (180g)
2 tablespoons olive oil
4 rashers rindless bacon (260g), sliced thinly
3 cups (480g) coarsely chopped barbecued chicken
1 large cos lettuce, trimmed, torn
6 green onions, sliced thinly
1 cup (80g) shaved parmesan cheese
caesar dressing
¾ cup (225g) whole-egg mayonnaise
1 tablespoon lemon juice
4 drained anchovy fillets, chopped finely
3 teaspoons dijon mustard
1 tablespoon water

1 Preheat oven to 180°C/160°C fan-forced.
2 Make caesar dressing.
3 Remove crusts from bread; discard crusts, cut bread into 2cm squares; toss with oil in medium bowl. Place bread, in single layer, on oven tray; toast in oven, 10 minutes.
4 Cook bacon in small frying pan, stirring, until browned and crisp. Drain on absorbent paper.
5 Place half of the chicken, half of the bacon, half of the croûtons and half of the dressing in large bowl with lettuce, half of the onion and half of the cheese; toss gently to combine.
6 Divide salad among serving plates. Top with remaining chicken, bacon, croûtons, onion and cheese; drizzle with remaining dressing.
caesar dressing blend or process ingredients until smooth.

preparation time 5 minutes **cooking time** 20 minutes **serves** 4
nutritional count per serving 49.9g total fat (12.3g saturated fat); 3390kJ (811 cal); 35.6g carbohydrate; 52.6g protein; 6.3g fibre

Lamb and fetta salad with warm walnut dressing

1 tablespoon vegetable oil
600g lamb fillets
200g fetta cheese, crumbled
250g witlof, trimmed, leaves separated
150g baby spinach leaves, trimmed
warm walnut dressing
2 cloves garlic, crushed
1 teaspoon finely grated lemon rind
¼ cup (60ml) olive oil
2 tablespoons cider vinegar
½ cup (55g) coarsely chopped roasted walnuts

1 Heat oil in large frying pan; cook lamb about 10 minutes.
Cover; stand 5 minutes then slice thickly.
2 Make warm walnut dressing.
3 Place lamb in medium bowl with cheese, witlof and spinach;
toss gently to combine. Serve salad drizzled with dressing.
warm walnut dressing stir garlic, rind, oil and vinegar in small
saucepan until hot. Remove from heat; stir in nuts.

preparation time 15 minutes **cooking time** 10 minutes **serves** 4
nutritional count per serving 52.8g total fat (16.8g saturated fat);
2742kJ (656 cal); 1.2g carbohydrate; 43.8g protein; 3.2g fibre

Hot and sour green papaya and pork salad

½ cup (125ml) water
600g pork fillets
1 small green papaya (650g)
1 large carrot (180g)
2 teaspoons vegetable oil
1 cup firmly packed fresh coriander leaves
⅓ cup (45g) coarsely chopped roasted unsalted peanuts
chilli and tamarind dressing
4 cloves garlic, crushed
4 fresh small red thai chillies, chopped finely
⅔ cup (200g) tamarind concentrate
1 tablespoon finely grated lime rind
½ cup (125ml) lime juice
2 shallots (50g), sliced thinly
⅓ cup grated palm sugar

1 Make chilli and tamarind dressing.
2 Place the water in large frying pan with ½ cup of the dressing. Add pork; bring to the boil. Reduce heat; simmer, covered, 20 minutes or until pork is cooked through. Remove pork from pan; cover, stand pork 10 minutes then slice thinly.
3 Peel then halve papaya; remove seeds. Using vegetable peeler, slice papaya and carrot lengthways into thin ribbons.
4 Stir oil into remaining dressing. Combine pork, papaya, carrot, coriander and dressing in medium bowl. Serve salad topped with nuts.
chilli and tamarind dressing combine ingredients in small jug.

preparation time 20 minutes **cooking time** 25 minutes **serves** 4
nutritional count per serving 11.4g total fat (2.3g saturated fat);
1643kJ (393 cal); 31.7g carbohydrate; 37.9g protein; 6.6g fibre

Lamb, spinach and spiced peach salad

20g butter
1 teaspoon ground coriander
½ teaspoon ground cardamom
¼ teaspoon ground cinnamon
3 medium peaches (450g), peeled, sliced thickly
2 tablespoons brown sugar
1 tablespoon raspberry vinegar
800g lamb backstrap
1 large red onion (300g), sliced thinly
150g snow peas, trimmed, sliced thinly
150g baby spinach leaves
2 fresh long red chillies, sliced thinly
raspberry dressing
120g raspberries
2 tablespoons raspberry vinegar
2 tablespoons olive oil
1 teaspoon sugar
1 teaspoon dijon mustard

1 Melt butter in large frying pan; cook spices, stirring, until fragrant. Add peach; cook, stirring, about 2 minutes or until just tender. Add sugar and vinegar; cook, stirring, until sugar dissolves. Remove peach from pan with slotted spoon; place in large bowl.
2 Add lamb to sugar mixture in pan; cook over low heat until browned both sides and cooked as desired. Cover lamb; stand 10 minutes then slice thickly.
3 Meanwhile, make raspberry dressing.
4 Add lamb and remaining ingredients to peaches; toss gently to combine. Serve salad drizzled with dressing.
raspberry dressing blend or process ingredients until smooth.

preparation time 20 minutes **cooking time** 15 minutes **serves** 4
nutritional count per serving 31.3g total fat (12g saturated fat);
2303kJ (551 cal); 21.3g carbohydrate; 46g protein; 5.6g fibre

Smoked chicken, radicchio and basil leaf salad

340g asparagus, trimmed, chopped coarsely
500g smoked chicken breast fillets, sliced thickly
2 medium radicchio (400g), trimmed, leaves torn
⅔ cup loosely packed fresh basil leaves
pesto dressing
2 teaspoons basil pesto
¼ cup (60ml) balsamic vinegar
¼ cup (60ml) olive oil

1 Boil, steam or microwave asparagus until tender; drain. Rinse under cold water; drain.
2 Meanwhile, make pesto dressing.
3 Place asparagus in large bowl with remaining ingredients and dressing; toss gently to combine.
pesto dressing place ingredients in screw-top jar; shake well.

preparation time 10 minutes   **cooking time** 5 minutes   **serves** 4
nutritional count per serving 23.8g total fat (4.6g saturated fat); 1513kJ (362 cal); 2g carbohydrate; 33.8g protein; 3.2g fibre

Five-spice pork and nashi in chilli plum dressing

600g pork fillets, trimmed
2 teaspoons vegetable oil
1 teaspoon five-spice powder
300g mizuna
2 green onions, sliced thinly
2 medium nashi (400g), sliced thinly
chilli plum dressing
¼ cup (60ml) plum sauce
1 tablespoon water
1 tablespoon lemon juice
1 fresh long red chilli, sliced thinly

1 Combine pork, oil and five-spice in large bowl. Cover; refrigerate 3 hours or overnight.
2 Make chilli plum dressing.
3 Cook pork on heated oiled grill plate (or grill or barbecue) for about 20 minutes. Cover; stand 10 minutes, then slice thickly.
4 Place mizuna, onion and nashi in large bowl with two-thirds of the dressing; toss gently to combine. Serve salad topped with pork, drizzled with remaining dressing.
chilli plum dressing place ingredients in screw-top jar; shake well.

preparation time 10 minutes (plus refrigeration time)
cooking time 20 minutes **serves** 4
nutritional count per serving 14.8g total fat (4.3g saturated fat); 1522kJ (364 cal); 22.5g carbohydrate; 33.3g protein; 3.1g fibre
tip nashi is a member of the pear family but resembles an apple with its pale-yellow-green, tennis-ball-sized appearance.

Greek-style wild rice salad with lemon and garlic yogurt

2 cups (400g) wild rice blend
1 medium red capsicum (200g)
1 medium brown onion (150g), quartered
250g cherry tomatoes
350g broccolini, halved crossways
½ cup (80g) roasted pine nuts
1 cup coarsely chopped fresh flat-leaf parsley
2 tablespoons lemon juice
lemon and garlic yogurt
2 cloves garlic, crushed
300g yogurt
¼ cup (60ml) lemon juice

1 Make lemon and garlic yogurt.
2 Cook rice in large saucepan of boiling water until tender; drain. Place in large serving bowl.
3 Quarter capsicum; discard seeds and membranes. Cook capsicum, onion and tomatoes on heated, oiled grill plate (or grill or barbecue) until tender. Chop capsicum and onion coarsely.
4 Boil, steam or microwave broccolini until tender.
5 Place rice, capsicum, onion and tomatoes in large serving bowl with nuts, parsley and juice; toss gently to combine. Serve salad topped with broccolini then yogurt.
lemon and garlic yogurt combine ingredients in small bowl.

preparation time 15 minutes **cooking time** 20 minutes **serves** 6
nutritional count per serving 11.6g total fat (1.7g saturated fat); 1007kJ (241 cal); 20.2g carbohydrate; 10.9g protein; 6.3g fibre

Crunchy cabbage, brazil nut and smoked chicken salad

800g smoked chicken breast fillets, sliced thinly
6 cups (480g) finely shredded wombok
1 medium red capsicum (200g), chopped coarsely
10 trimmed red radishes (150g), sliced thinly
4 green onions, sliced thinly
¼ cup coarsely chopped fresh coriander
¼ cup coarsely chopped fresh flat-leaf parsley
½ cup (80g) roasted brazil nuts, chopped coarsely
chilli lime dressing
¼ cup (60ml) lime juice
1 fresh long red chilli, chopped finely
1 tablespoon grated palm sugar
2 tablespoons fish sauce
2 teaspoons sesame oil

1 Make chilli lime dressing.
2 Place chicken in large bowl with remaining salad ingredients and dressing; toss gently to combine.
chilli lime dressing place ingredients in screw-top jar; shake well.

preparation time 20 minutes **serves** 4
nutritional count per serving 30.2g total fat (7.3g saturated fat); 2240kJ (536 cal); 8.3g carbohydrate; 55.6g protein; 4.8g fibre

Orange, beetroot and roast beef salad

2 medium oranges (480g)
½ cup (125ml) buttermilk
¼ cup (75g) mayonnaise
1 tablespoon wholegrain mustard
400g shaved rare roast beef
850g can whole baby beetroot, drained, halved
150g baby rocket leaves
100g blue cheese, crumbled

1 Segment oranges over large bowl; reserve 1 tablespoon juice in small bowl.
2 Whisk buttermilk, mayonnaise and mustard into juice.
3 Add beef, beetroot and rocket to large bowl; toss gently to combine. Sprinkle cheese over salad; drizzle with dressing.

preparation time 15 minutes **serves** 4
nutritional count per serving 19.9g total fat (8.4g saturated fat); 1860kJ (445 cal); 26.8g carbohydrate; 36.4g protein; 6.2g fibre

Thai pork salad with kaffir lime dressing

600g pork fillets
2 tablespoons grated palm sugar
1 tablespoon finely grated lime rind
2 teaspoons peanut oil
350g watercress, trimmed
1 cup loosely packed fresh thai basil leaves
½ cup loosely packed fresh coriander leaves
½ cup loosely packed fresh mint leaves
1½ cups (120g) bean sprouts
1 medium green capsicum (200g), sliced thinly
kaffir lime dressing
2 cloves garlic, crushed
3 shallots (75g), sliced thinly
1 fresh small red thai chilli, sliced thinly
3 fresh kaffir lime leaves, sliced thinly
¼ cup (60ml) lime juice
⅓ cup (80ml) fish sauce
2 teaspoons grated palm sugar

1 Cut pork fillets in half horizontally. Combine sugar, rind and oil in large bowl with pork.
2 Cook pork mixture, in batches, in heated oiled large frying pan, over medium heat, about 15 minutes or until cooked through. Cover pork; stand 5 minutes, then slice thinly.
3 Meanwhile, make kaffir lime dressing.
4 Place pork in large bowl with remaining ingredients and dressing; toss gently to combine.
kaffir lime dressing place ingredients in screw-top jar; shake well.

preparation time 15 minutes **cooking time** 15 minutes **serves** 4
nutritional count per serving 6.4g total fat (1.6g saturated fat);
1104kJ (264 cal); 12.2g carbohydrate; 38.8g protein; 5.8g fibre

Blt salad

250g cherry tomatoes
cooking-oil spray
6 rashers rindless bacon (390g)
1 small french bread stick (150g)
180g bocconcini cheese, halved
1 large cos lettuce, leaves separated, torn
mustard mayonnaise
⅓ cup (100g) mayonnaise
2 teaspoons wholegrain mustard
¼ cup (60ml) lemon juice

1 Preheat grill. Make mustard mayonnaise.
2 Place tomatoes on oven tray; spray with oil. Grill until softened slightly. Cover to keep warm.
3 Grill bacon until crisp. Chop coarsely.
4 Cut bread into 8 slices; toast under grill until browned both sides.
5 Place half of the tomato and half of the bacon in large bowl with half of the cheese and all the lettuce; toss gently to combine.
6 Divide salad among serving dishes; sprinkle with remaining tomato, bacon and cheese. Serve salad with toast; drizzle with mayonnaise.
mustard mayonnaise combine ingredients in small bowl.

preparation time 10 minutes **cooking time** 15 minutes **serves** 4
nutritional count per serving 31.2g total fat (16.4g saturated fat); 2312kJ (553 cal); 31.1g carbohydrate; 33.9g protein; 7.1g fibre

Roasted kumara, cranberry, chicken and spinach salad

1 large kumara (500g), cut into 2cm pieces
1 medium red onion (170g), cut into wedges
1 tablespoon maple syrup
1 tablespoon olive oil
600g chicken breast fillets
80g baby spinach leaves
⅓ cup (45g) dried cranberries
⅓ cup (50g) pine nuts
cranberry dressing
2 tablespoons olive oil
¼ cup (80g) whole berry cranberry sauce, warmed
1 tablespoon red wine vinegar

1 Preheat oven to 220°C/200°C fan-forced.
2 Combine kumara, onion, syrup and oil in large shallow baking dish; roast about 35 minutes or until vegetables are tender, stirring halfway through roasting time.
3 Meanwhile, make cranberry dressing.
4 Cook chicken in heated oiled medium frying pan until cooked through. Remove from pan; slice thickly.
5 Place kumara mixture and chicken in medium bowl with spinach, cranberries, nuts and half of the dressing; toss gently to combine. Divide salad among serving plates; drizzle with remaining dressing.
cranberry dressing whisk ingredients in small jug to combine.

preparation time 10 minutes **cooking time** 35 minutes **serves** 4
nutritional count per serving 30.9g total fat (5g saturated fat);
2449kJ (586 cal); 37.7g carbohydrate; 37.2g protein; 4.3g fibre

Grilled lamb and lebanese chickpea salad

3 cloves garlic, crushed
¼ cup (60ml) lemon juice
1 tablespoon olive oil
2 teaspoons ground cumin
750g lamb backstraps
2 tablespoons lemon juice, extra
2 tablespoons olive oil, extra
800g can chickpeas, rinsed, drained
3 medium egg tomatoes (225g), cut into wedges
1 lebanese cucumber (130g), halved lengthways, sliced thinly
1 medium red onion (170g), sliced thinly
½ cup coarsely chopped fresh mint
½ cup coarsely chopped fresh flat-leaf parsley

1 Combine garlic, juice, oil and cumin in large bowl with lamb. Cover; refrigerate 3 hours or overnight.
2 Drain lamb; reserve marinade. Cook lamb on heated, oiled grill plate (or grill or barbecue), brushing occasionally with marinade. Cover lamb; stand 5 minutes, then slice thinly.
3 Whisk extra juice and extra oil in large bowl, add remaining ingredients; toss gently to combine. Serve salad topped with lamb.

preparation time 15 minutes (plus refrigeration time)
cooking time 10 minutes   **serves** 4
nutritional count per serving 33.2g total fat (9.8g saturated fat); 2537kJ (607 cal); 23.3g carbohydrate; 49.5g protein; 9.1g fibre

Honey soy chicken salad

You need about a quarter of a small savoy cabbage for this recipe.

⅓ cup (115g) honey
2 tablespoons soy sauce
1 clove garlic, crushed
4 small fresh red thai chillies, seeded, chopped finely
600g chicken breast fillets, sliced thinly
300g snow peas
1 small carrot (120g)
1 tablespoon peanut oil
2 cups (160g) finely shredded savoy cabbage
1 medium yellow capsicum (200g), sliced thinly
1 medium red capsicum (200g), sliced thinly
1 lebanese cucumber (130g), seeded, sliced thinly
4 green onions, sliced thinly
½ cup loosely packed fresh mint leaves
2 tablespoons lime juice
2 teaspoons sesame oil

1 Combine honey, sauce, garlic and half of the chilli in medium bowl with chicken. Cover; refrigerate until required.
2 Boil, steam or microwave snow peas until just tender; drain. Rinse immediately under cold water; drain. Using vegetable peeler, slice carrot into thin ribbons.
3 Heat peanut oil in wok; stir-fry drained chicken, in batches, until browned and cooked through.
4 Place chicken, snow peas and carrot in large serving bowl with remaining ingredients and remaining chilli; toss gently to combine.

preparation time 20 mintues (plus refrigeration time)
cooking time 10 mintues **serves** 4
nutritional count per serving 10.8g total fat (2.1g saturated fat); 1701kJ (407 cal); 34.2g carbohydrate; 39.6g protein; 5.9g fibre
tip you can use a large barbecued chicken instead of the breast fillets; discard bones and skin, then shred meat coarsely before tossing with remaining salad ingredients.

Panzanella

1 litre (4 cups) water
250g stale sourdough bread, cut into 2cm slices
2 large tomatoes (440g), chopped coarsely
1 small red onion (100g), sliced thinly
2 lebanese cucumbers (260g), chopped coarsely
1 cup firmly packed fresh basil leaves
2 tablespoons olive oil
2 tablespoons red wine vinegar
1 clove garlic, crushed

1 Place the water in large shallow bowl; briefly dip bread slices into water. Pat dry with absorbent paper; tear bread into large chunks.
2 Place bread in large bowl with remaining ingredients; toss gently to combine.

preparation time 20 minutes **serves** 4
nutritional count per serving 11g total fat (1.5g saturated fat); 1104kJ (264 cal); 33.2g carbohydrate; 7.5g protein; 6g fibre

Kaffir lime and rice salad with tofu and cashews

2 cups (400g) jasmine rice
2 fresh kaffir lime leaves, chopped finely
2 fresh long red chillies, chopped finely
2cm piece fresh ginger (10g), grated
400g packaged marinated tofu pieces, sliced thickly
½ cup coarsely chopped fresh coriander
1 large carrot (180g), cut into matchsticks
3 green onions, sliced thinly
¾ cup (120g) roasted unsalted cashews, chopped coarsely
lime and palm sugar dressing
1 teaspoon finely grated lime rind
½ cup (125ml) lime juice
2 tablespoons grated palm sugar
2 tablespoons fish sauce

1 Cook rice in large saucepan of boiling water until tender; drain. Rinse under cold water; drain.
2 Meanwhile, make lime and palm sugar dressing.
3 Place rice in large bowl with lime leaves, chilli, ginger, tofu, coriander, carrot, half of the onion, ½ cup nuts and dressing; toss gently to combine. Serve salad sprinkled with remaining onion and nuts.
lime and palm sugar dressing place ingredients in screw-top jar; shake well.

preparation time 20 minutes **cooking time** 10 minutes **serves** 4
nutritional count per serving 22.2g total fat (3.7g saturated fat); 2847kJ (681 cal); 90.9g carbohydrate; 25.6g protein; 6.3g fibre
tip we used a cryovac-packed ready-to-serve sweet chilli tofu in this recipe; there are various flavours of already marinated tofu pieces that can be found in the refrigerated section of most supermarkets and Asian food stores.

Oak leaf and mixed herb salad with dijon vinaigrette

1 green oak leaf lettuce, leaves separated
¼ cup coarsely chopped fresh chives
½ cup firmly packed fresh flat-leaf parsley leaves
½ cup firmly packed fresh chervil leaves
dijon vinaigrette
2 tablespoons olive oil
2 tablespoons white wine vinegar
1 tablespoon dijon mustard
2 teaspoons white sugar

1 Make dijon vinaigrette.
2 Place salad ingredients in medium bowl with dressing; toss gently to combine.
dijon vinaigrette place ingredients in screw-top jar; shake well.

preparation time 10 minutes **serves** 6
nutritional count per serving 6.2g total fat (0.9g saturated fat); 288kJ (69 cal); 2g carbohydrate; 0.7g protein; 1.1g fibre

Warm crunchy rice salad

1 cup (200g) wild rice blend
1 medium red capsicum (200g), sliced thinly
1 small red onion (100g), sliced thinly
⅓ cup (50g) sunflower seed kernels
⅓ cup (65g) pepitas
⅓ cup (50g) roasted unsalted cashews
½ cup coarsely chopped fresh flat-leaf parsley
2 tablespoons coarsely chopped fresh oregano
black pepper dressing
1 teaspoon finely grated lemon rind
¼ cup (60ml) lemon juice
2 tablespoons olive oil
1 teaspoon dijon mustard
1 teaspoon cracked black pepper

1 Cook rice in large saucepan of boiling water until just tender; drain.
Rinse under warm water; drain.
2 Meanwhile, make black pepper dressing.
3 Place rice in large bowl with remaining salad ingredients and dressing;
toss gently to combine.
black pepper dressing place ingredients in screw-top jar; shake well.

preparation time 15 minutes **cooking time** 10 minutes **serves** 4
nutritional count per serving 27.4g total fat (2.9g saturated fat);
1639kJ (392 cal); 15.7g carbohydrate; 8.3g protein; 6g fibre

Potato salad

2kg potatoes, peeled
2 tablespoons cider vinegar
4 green onions, sliced thinly
¼ cup finely chopped fresh flat-leaf parsley
mayonnaise
2 egg yolks
2 teaspoons lemon juice
1 teaspoon dijon mustard
1 cup (250ml) vegetable oil
2 tablespoons warm water, approximately

1 Cover potatoes with cold water in large saucepan; bring to the boil. Reduce heat; simmer, covered, until tender. Drain; cut into 3cm pieces. Spread potato on a tray, sprinkle with vinegar; refrigerate until cold.
2 Make mayonnaise.
3 Place potato in large bowl with onion, parsley and mayonnaise; toss gently to combine.
mayonnaise blend or process egg yolks, juice and mustard until smooth. With motor operating, gradually add oil in a thin, steady stream; process until mixture thickens. Add as much of the warm water as required to thin mayonnaise.

preparation time 30 minutes (plus refrigeration time)
cooking time 15 minutes **serves** 8
nutritional count per serving 30.4g total fat (4.1g saturated fat); 1764kJ (422 cal); 29g carbohydrate; 6.2g protein; 3.7g fibre
tip everyone has a different opinion as to what a potato salad should be – served hot or cold, creamy or dressed with a vinaigrette, with bacon bits or simply sprinkled with fresh herbs – but you'd be hard-pressed to find one you didn't like. Cover the saucepan while potatoes are cooking, but lift the lid and give them an occasional gentle stir to move them around. Don't overcook them or they will break apart or crumble.

Italian-style bean salad with mozzarella, sun-dried tomato and olives

200g green beans, trimmed, halved crossways
2 x 420g cans four-bean mix, rinsed, drained
2 teaspoons finely chopped fresh thyme
2 teaspoons finely chopped fresh oregano
⅓ cup coarsely chopped fresh flat-leaf parsley
100g mozzarella cheese, sliced thickly
¾ cup (110g) drained sun-dried tomatoes, sliced thinly
1 medium brown onion (150g), sliced thinly
1 cup (120g) seeded black olives
italian dressing
1 clove garlic, crushed
2 tablespoons olive oil
2 tablespoons lemon juice

1 Boil, steam or microwave green beans until tender; drain. Rinse under cold water; drain.
2 Meanwhile, make italian dressing.
3 Place green beans and four-bean mix in medium bowl with remaining salad ingredients and dressing; toss gently to combine.
italian dressing place ingredients in screw-top jar; shake well.

preparation time 15 minutes **cooking time** 5 minutes **serves** 4
nutritional count per serving 16.6g total fat (5.1g saturated fat); 1438kJ (344 cal); 28g carbohydrate; 15.6g protein; 10.5g fibre

Green and yellow split pea salad with wholegrain mustard dressing

½ cup (100g) yellow split peas
½ cup (100g) green split peas
4 green onions, sliced thinly
250g cherry tomatoes, halved
½ cup coarsely chopped fresh flat-leaf parsley
wholegrain mustard dressing
¼ cup (60ml) lemon juice
¼ cup (60ml) olive oil
1 tablespoon wholegrain mustard
2 cloves garlic, crushed

1 Place peas in medium bowl, cover with cold water; stand overnight, drain. Rinse under cold water; drain.
2 Place peas in medium saucepan, cover with boiling water. Simmer, covered, about 10 minutes or until peas are tender; rinse under cold water, drain.
3 Make wholegrain mustard dressing.
4 Place peas in large bowl with remaining salad ingredients and dressing; toss gently to combine.
wholegrain mustard dressing whisk ingredients in small bowl.

preparation time 10 minutes (plus standing time)
cooking time 20 minutes **serves** 6
nutritional count per serving 9.9g total fat (1.4g saturated fat); 836kJ (200 cal); 17.3g carbohydrate; 8.3g protein; 4.7g fibre

Caesar salad

½ loaf ciabatta (220g)
1 clove garlic, crushed
⅓ cup (80ml) olive oil
2 eggs
3 baby cos lettuces (540g), leaves separated
1 cup (80g) shaved parmesan cheese
caesar dressing
1 clove garlic, crushed
1 tablespoon dijon mustard
2 tablespoons lemon juice
2 teaspoons worcestershire sauce
2 tablespoons olive oil

1 Preheat oven to 180°C/160°C fan-forced.

2 Cut bread into 2cm cubes. Combine garlic and oil in large bowl with bread. Place bread, in single layer, on oven trays; toast in oven about 15 minutes or until croûtons are browned lightly.

3 Bring water to the boil in small saucepan; using slotted spoon, carefully lower whole eggs into water. Cover pan tightly, remove from heat; using same slotted spoon, remove eggs from water after 1 minute. When cool enough to handle, break eggs into large bowl, add lettuce; toss gently to combine. Add cheese and croûtons.

4 Make caesar dressing.

5 Pour dressing over salad; toss gently to combine.

caesar dressing place ingredients in screw-top jar; shake well.

preparation time 30 minutes **cooking time** 20 minutes **serves** 4
nutritional count per serving 38.4g total fat (9g saturated fat); 2195kJ (525 cal); 28g carbohydrate; 17.7g protein; 4.6g fibre
tip named after Caesar Cardini, the Italian-American who tossed the first Caesar in his restaurant in Tijuana, Mexico, during the 1920s, this salad must always contain – as authenticated by Cardini's daughter – freshly made garlic croutons, crisp cos lettuce leaves, coddled eggs, lemon juice, olive oil, worcestershire sauce, black pepper and parmesan... no single ingredient is meant to dominate. The original Caesar didn't contain bacon, hard-boiled egg, chicken breast or anchovies (the worcestershire sauce gave it that anchovy flavour).

Coleslaw

½ small cabbage (600g), shredded finely
1 medium carrot (120g), grated coarsely
4 green onions, sliced thinly
½ cup (150g) mayonnaise
1 tablespoon lemon juice

1 Place cabbage, carrot and onion in large bowl with combined mayonnaise and juice; toss gently to combine.

preparation time 10 minutes **serves** 6
nutritional count per serving 8.1g total fat (1g saturated fat); 523kJ (125 cal); 8.8g carbohydrate; 2g protein; 4.5g fibre
tips you can use any cabbage variety for coleslaw − red, savoy, even wombok − but we chose to shred a traditional firm, white drumhead in our recipe. After trimming a cabbage, cut it into manageable-size wedges to make shredding it finely a lot easier.

Pear, walnut and fetta salad with walnut dressing

1 butter lettuce
1 medium pear (230g), cored
⅓ cup (35g) roasted walnuts, chopped coarsely
40g snow pea sprouts, trimmed
50g fetta cheese, crumbled
35g shaved parmesan cheese
walnut dressing
1 tablespoon walnut oil
2 teaspoons wholegrain mustard
2 tablespoons white wine vinegar
1 tablespoon finely chopped fresh chives

1 Make walnut dressing.
2 Separate lettuce leaves; tear leaves roughly.
3 Slice unpeeled pear into thin wedges.
4 Place lettuce and pear in large bowl with remaining salad ingredients and dressing; toss gently to combine.
walnut dressing place ingredients in screw-top jar; shake well.

preparation time 20 minutes **serves** 4
nutritional count per serving 16.6g total fat (5g saturated fat); 957kJ (229 cal); 10.4g carbohydrate; 8.4g protein; 3.3g fibre

Pasta salad

250g orecchiette pasta
2 tablespoons drained sun-dried tomatoes, chopped coarsely
1 small red onion (100g), sliced thinly
1 small green capsicum (150g), sliced thinly
½ cup coarsely chopped fresh flat-leaf parsley
sun-dried tomato dressing
1 tablespoon sun-dried tomato pesto
1 tablespoon white wine vinegar
2 tablespoons olive oil

1 Cook pasta in large saucepan of boiling water until just tender; drain.
Rinse under cold water; drain.
2 Make sun-dried tomato dressing.
3 Place pasta in large bowl with remaining salad ingredients and
dressing; toss gently to combine.
sun-dried tomato dressing place ingredients in screw-top jar; shake well.

preparation time 15 minutes **cooking time** 10 minutes **serves** 4
nutritional count per serving 12g total fat (1.9g saturated fat);
1405kJ (336 cal); 46g carbohydrate; 8.8g protein; 3.6g fibre
tip pasta salad is another one of those favourites that has as many
versions as there are cooks who make it. Because it's eaten cold,
it's ideal for picnics or lunchboxes, and as a side salad with a simple
midweek meal of grilled chops.

Chickpea salad

1½ cups (300g) dried chickpeas
250g cherry tomatoes, halved
1 large green cucumber (400g), seeded, chopped coarsely
1 medium red onion (170g), chopped finely
¼ cup finely shredded fresh mint leaves
dressing
¼ cup (60ml) lime juice
¼ cup (60ml) olive oil
2 teaspoons dijon mustard
¼ teaspoon sugar
2 cloves garlic, crushed

1 Place chickpeas in large bowl; cover with water. Soak overnight; drain.
2 Cook chickpeas in large saucepan of boiling water about 50 minutes or until tender; drain. Rinse under cold water; drain.
3 Make dressing.
4 Place chickpeas in large bowl with remaining salad ingredients and dressing; toss gently to combine.
dressing place ingredients in screw-top jar; shake well.

preparation time 20 minutes (plus standing time)
cooking time 50 minutes **serves** 8
nutritional count per serving 9.2g total fat (1.3g saturated fat); 786kJ (188 cal); 16.3g carbohydrate; 7.3g protein; 6g fibre
tips you can use canned rather than dried chickpeas in this recipe. Rinse two 400g cans of chickpeas well under cold water; drain well before combining with other ingredients.
This recipe can be made a day ahead and refrigerated, covered, overnight.

Waldorf salad

4 medium red apples (600g)
¼ cup (60ml) lemon juice
5 trimmed celery stalks (500g), chopped coarsely
1 cup (110g) coarsely chopped roasted walnuts
mayonnaise
2 egg yolks
2 teaspoons lemon juice
1 teaspoon dijon mustard
¾ cup (180ml) olive oil
1 tablespoon warm water

1 Make mayonnaise.
2 Core unpeeled apples; cut into wedges.
3 Place apples in large serving bowl with remaining salad ingredients and mayonnaise; toss gently to combine.
mayonnaise blend or process egg yolks, juice and mustard until smooth. With motor operating, gradually add oil in a thin, steady stream; process until mixture thickens. Add as much of the warm water as required to thin mayonnaise.

preparation time 15 minutes **serves** 4
nutritional count per serving 63.1g total fat (7.8g saturated fat); 2800kJ (670 cal); 17.8g carbohydrate; 6.8g protein; 6.5g fibre

Pasta salad with fried sprouts, bocconcini and almonds

500g rigatoni pasta
1 tablespoon olive oil
300g brussels sprouts, trimmed, shredded
½ cup coarsely chopped fresh flat-leaf parsley
1 tablespoon drained capers, rinsed
200g bocconcini cheese, sliced thickly
½ cup (80g) roasted almonds, chopped coarsely
red wine vinaigrette
⅓ cup (80ml) lemon juice
⅓ cup (80ml) red wine vinegar
¼ cup (60ml) olive oil
1 teaspoon white sugar
2 cloves garlic, crushed

1 Make red wine vinaigrette.
2 Cook pasta in large saucepan of boiling water until just tender; drain. Place in large serving bowl.
3 Heat oil in same pan; stir-fry sprouts about 1 minute or until just warm.
4 Place pasta and sprouts in large bowl with remaining salad ingredients and vinaigrette; toss gently to combine.
red wine vinaigrette place ingredients in screw-top jar; shake well.

preparation time 20 minutes **cooking time** 15 minutes **serves** 6
nutritional count per serving 25.7g total fat (5.7g saturated fat); 2358kJ (564 cal); 60g carbohydrate; 19.9g protein; 6.2g fibre

Moroccan couscous salad with preserved lemon dressing

1½ cups (300g) couscous
1½ cups (375ml) boiling water
20g butter
420g can chickpeas, rinsed, drained
⅓ cup (55g) sultanas
⅓ cup (50g) roasted pine nuts
100g baby rocket leaves, chopped coarsely
¾ cup finely chopped fresh flat-leaf parsley
1 cup (120g) seeded green olives
preserved lemon dressing
1 tablespoon finely grated lemon rind
¼ cup (60ml) lemon juice
¼ cup (60ml) olive oil
2 tablespoons rinsed and drained finely chopped preserved lemon

1 Combine couscous and the water in large heatproof bowl, cover; stand about 5 minutes or until water is absorbed, fluffing with fork occasionally. Stir in butter. Stand 10 minutes.
2 Make preserved lemon dressing.
3 Add remaining salad ingredients and dressing to couscous; toss gently to combine.
preserved lemon dressing place ingredients in screw-top jar; shake well.

preparation time 20 minutes **serves** 4
nutritional count per serving 29g total fat (5.5g saturated fat); 268kJ (686 cal); 85.6g carbohydrate; 17.2g protein; 6.5g fibre
tip preserved lemon is a North African speciality, where lemons, whole or sliced, are placed in a mixture of salt and oil or lemon juice. Rinsed well, the peel can be chopped and stirred into a salad dressing, or added to a simmering casserole or tagine for extra piquancy. Preserved lemons are available from specialist food shops and delicatessens.

Thai herb and mango salad

2 medium mangoes (860g)
10cm stick (20g) fresh lemon grass, sliced thinly
2 fresh long red chillies, cut into thin strips
150g snow peas, trimmed, sliced thinly
6 green onions, sliced thinly
1 cup (80g) bean sprouts
½ cup loosely packed fresh coriander leaves
¼ cup loosely packed fresh mint leaves
¼ cup loosely packed vietnamese mint leaves
1 tablespoon coarsely shredded thai basil
palm sugar and lime dressing
¼ cup (60ml) lime juice
1 tablespoon fish sauce
2 tablespoons grated palm sugar
2 cloves garlic, crushed

1 Make palm sugar and lime dressing.
2 Slice cheeks from mangoes; cut each cheek into thin strips.
3 Place mango in large bowl with remaining salad ingredients and dressing; toss gently to combine.
palm sugar and lime dressing place ingredients in screw-top jar; shake well.

preparation time 25 minutes **serves** 4
nutritional count per serving 0.6g total fat (0g saturated fat); 631kJ (151 cal); 29.3g carbohydrate; 4.5g protein; 5g fibre

Pepita and oak leaf lettuce salad with cranberry dressing

1 green oak leaf lettuce, leaves separated
1 small red onion (100g), sliced thinly
⅓ cup (65g) roasted pepitas
cranberry dressing
2 tablespoons olive oil
2 tablespoons red wine vinegar
2 tablespoons cranberry sauce

1 Make cranberry dressing.
2 Place salad ingredients in medium bowl with dressing; toss gently to combine.
cranberry dressing place ingredients in screw-top jar; shake well.

preparation time 10 minutes **serves** 6
nutritional count per serving 9.8g total fat (0.9g saturated fat); 464kJ (111 cal); 4.4g carbohydrate; 0.7g protein; 2g fibre

165

Thai herb and mango salad

2 medium mangoes (860g)
10cm stick (20g) fresh lemon grass, sliced thinly
2 fresh long red chillies, cut into thin strips
150g snow peas, trimmed, sliced thinly
6 green onions, sliced thinly
1 cup (80g) bean sprouts
½ cup loosely packed fresh coriander leaves
¼ cup loosely packed fresh mint leaves
¼ cup loosely packed vietnamese mint leaves
1 tablespoon coarsely shredded thai basil
palm sugar and lime dressing
¼ cup (60ml) lime juice
1 tablespoon fish sauce
2 tablespoons grated palm sugar
2 cloves garlic, crushed

1 Make palm sugar and lime dressing.
2 Slice cheeks from mangoes; cut each cheek into thin strips.
3 Place mango in large bowl with remaining salad ingredients and dressing; toss gently to combine.
palm sugar and lime dressing place ingredients in screw-top jar; shake well.

preparation time 25 minutes **serves** 4
nutritional count per serving 0.6g total fat (0g saturated fat); 631kJ (151 cal); 29.3g carbohydrate; 4.5g protein; 5g fibre

Tabbouleh

¼ cup (40g) burghul
3 medium tomatoes (450g)
3 cups coarsely chopped fresh flat-leaf parsley
3 green onions, chopped finely
¼ cup coarsely chopped fresh mint
¼ cup (60ml) lemon juice
¼ cup (60ml) olive oil

1 Place burghul in medium shallow bowl. Halve tomatoes, scoop pulp from tomato over burghul. Chop tomato flesh finely; spread over burghul. Cover; refrigerate 1 hour.
2 Combine burghul mixture in large bowl with remaining ingredients.

preparation time 30 minutes (plus refrigeration time) **serves** 4
nutritional count per serving 14.1g total fat (2g saturated fat);
790kJ (189 cal); 9.2g carbohydrate; 3.4g protein; 5.6g fibre
tip tabbouleh is traditionally made with a great deal of chopped flat-leaf parsley and varying smaller amounts of burghul, green onion and mint. Go easy on the burghul: too much and the completed tabbouleh will be overly heavy instead of fluffy and light as it is meant to be.

Green bean and tomato salad with mustard hazelnut dressing

200g green beans, trimmed
250g cherry tomatoes, halved
mustard hazelnut dressing
½ cup (70g) roasted hazelnuts, skinned, chopped coarsely
2 tablespoons hazelnut oil
2 tablespoons cider vinegar
1 teaspoon wholegrain mustard

1 Make mustard hazelnut dressing.
2 Boil, steam or microwave beans until tender; drain. Rinse under cold water; drain.
3 Palce beans and tomatoes in medium bowl with dressing; toss gently to combine.
mustard hazelnut dressing place ingredients in screw-top jar; shake well.

preparation time 10 minutes **cooking time** 10 minutes **serves** 4
nutritional count per serving 20.2g total fat (1.8g saturated fat); 920kJ (220 cal); 3.6g carbohydrate; 4.2g protein; 4.3g fibre

Three-cabbage coleslaw with shredded chicken

You need about half a small wombok, a quarter of a savoy cabbage and a quarter of a red cabbage for this recipe.

3 cups (480g) shredded barbecued chicken
3 cups (240g) finely shredded wombok
3 cups (240g) finely shredded savoy cabbage
3 cups (240g) finely shredded red cabbage
2 medium carrots (240g), grated coarsely
1 medium green capsicum (200g), sliced thinly
¼ cup finely chopped fresh dill
fennel slaw dressing
½ cup (140g) yogurt
⅓ cup (100g) mayonnaise
⅓ cup (80ml) cider vinegar
1 small brown onion (80g), grated coarsely
2 teaspoons white sugar
2 teaspoons fennel seeds

1 Make fennel slaw dressing.
2 Place salad ingredients in large bowl with dressing; toss gently to combine. Refrigerate, covered, at least 1 hour.
fennel slaw dressing combine ingredients in small bowl.

preparation time 20 minutes (plus refrigeration time) **serves** 6
nutritional count per serving 12.4g total fat (2.9g saturated fat); 1095kJ (262 cal); 11.3g carbohydrate; 23.7g protein; 5g fibre

173

Rocket, parmesan and semi-dried tomato salad

100g baby rocket leaves
2 tablespoons roasted pine nuts
40g drained semi-dried tomatoes, chopped coarsely
⅓ cup (25g) shaved parmesan cheese
1 tablespoon olive oil
1 tablespoon balsamic vinegar

1 Place rocket, nuts, tomato and cheese in large bowl with combined oil and vinegar; toss gently to combine.

preparation time 10 minutes **serves** 4
nutritional count per serving 12.3g total fat (2.3g saturated fat); 635kJ (152 cal); 4.4g carbohydrate; 5.1g protein; 2.2g fibre

Greek salad

4 medium egg tomatoes (300g), sliced thinly
2 lebanese cucumbers (260g), chopped coarsely
1 small red onion (100g), sliced thinly
½ cup (75g) seeded kalamata olives
150g fetta cheese, chopped coarsely
dressing
2 tablespoons olive oil
2 tablespoons lemon juice
2 teaspoons fresh oregano leaves

1 Make dressing.
2 Place tomato, cucumber, onion, olives and cheese in large bowl;
toss gently to combine. Drizzle dressing over salad.
dressing place ingredients in screw-top jar; shake well.

preparation time 15 minutes **serves** 4
nutritional count per serving 18.2g total fat (7.1g saturated fat);
991kJ (237 cal); 9g carbohydrate; 8.3g protein; 2.4g fibre
tip this crunchy salad is found on tables all over the world, not just in
Greece. The only obligatory ingredients are fetta, tomato and onion; use
your imagination and add capers, hard-boiled eggs, and red or green
capsicum – as long as it offers "bite", the sky's the limit.

Three-bean salad with lemon chilli breadcrumbs

150g green beans, trimmed
150g yellow beans, trimmed
300g frozen broad beans
2 tablespoons olive oil
2 tablespoons lemon juice
lemon chilli breadcrumbs
25g butter
1 tablespoon finely grated lemon rind
⅓ cup (25g) stale breadcrumbs
¼ teaspoon chilli powder

1 Make lemon chilli breadcrumbs.
2 Boil, steam or microwave green, yellow and broad beans, separately, until tender; drain. Rinse under cold water; drain. Peel away grey outer shells from broad beans.
3 Place all beans in medium bowl with oil and juice; toss gently to combine. Serve sprinkled with breadcrumbs.
lemon chilli breadcrumbs melt butter in small frying pan; cook remaining ingredients over low heat, stirring, until crumbs are browned.

preparation time 5 minutes **cooking time** 20 minutes **serves** 6
nutritional count per serving 10g total fat (3.2g saturated fat); 594kJ (142 cal);5.3g carbohydrate; 5.2g protein; 4.8g fibre

Chipotle, corn, tomato and chickpea salad

1 chipotle chilli
2 tablespoons boiling water
½ cup (130g) bottled tomato pasta sauce
1 tablespoon lime juice
1 teaspoon ground cumin
2 trimmed corn cobs (500g)
420g can chickpeas, drained, rinsed
250g cherry tomatoes, halved
1 small red onion (100g), sliced thinly
1 cup loosely packed fresh coriander leaves

1 Place chilli and the water in small bowl; stand 15 minutes. Discard stalk; blend or process chilli, soaking liquid with pasta sauce until smooth. Transfer to small bowl; stir in juice.
2 Dry-fry cumin in small frying pan, stirring, until fragrant; stir into chilli sauce mixture.
3 Cook corn on heated oiled grill plate (or grill or barbecue) until browned lightly and tender. Cut kernels from cobs.
4 Combine chilli mixture and corn in large bowl with remaining ingredients.

preparation time 20 minutes (plus standing time)
cooking time 15 minutes **serves** 4
nutritional count per serving 2.9g total fat (0.3g saturated fat);
853kJ (204 cal); 30.5g carbohydrate; 9.5g protein; 9.4g fibre

Cauliflower and green olive salad

1 small cauliflower (1kg), trimmed, cut into florets
1 cup (120g) large green olives, seeded, halved
1 trimmed celery stalk (100g), sliced thinly
1 cup loosely packed celery leaves
½ cup loosely packed fresh flat-leaf parsley leaves
1 small red onion (100g), sliced thinly
2 tablespoons lemon juice
1 tablespoon finely chopped preserved lemon
2 tablespoons olive oil
1 clove garlic, crushed
125g fetta cheese, crumbled

1 Boil, steam or microwave cauliflower until tender; drain.
2 Place cauliflower in medium bowl with olives, celery, celery leaves, parsley, onion, juice, preserved lemon, oil and garlic; toss gently to combine.
3 Serve salad sprinkled with cheese.

preparation time 15 minutes **cooking time** 5 minutes **serves** 4
nutritional count per serving 17.2g total fat (6.1g saturated fat);
1087kJ (260 cal); 12.3g carbohydrate; 11.3g protein; 5.5g fibre
tips in this recipe, we used only the leaves from the inner stalks of
celery. Pale in colour, these are not bitter as are the tougher outer leaves.
Preserved lemons, salted lemons preserved in a mixture of olive oil and
lemon juice, are available from specialty food shops and delicatessens.

Green papaya salad

You need a small fresh coconut for this recipe.

10cm stick fresh lemon grass (20g)
1 small green papaya (650g)
2 cups (160g) bean sprouts
1 cup (100g) coarsely grated fresh coconut
¾ cup loosely packed fresh coriander leaves
¾ cup loosely packed fresh mint leaves
2 purple shallots (50g), sliced thinly
½ cup (70g) roasted unsalted peanuts, chopped coarsely
chilli citrus dressing
¼ cup (60ml) lime juice
¼ cup (60ml) lemon juice
1 tablespoon grated palm sugar
2 teaspoons fish sauce
1 fresh small red thai chilli, chopped finely

1 Soak lemon grass in medium heatproof bowl of boiling water
about 4 minutes or until tender. Drain; slice lemon grass thinly.
2 Meanwhile, make chilli citrus dressing.
3 Peel papaya, quarter lengthways, discard seeds; grate papaya
flesh coarsely.
4 Place lemon grass and papaya in large bowl with sprouts, coconut,
herbs, shallots and dressing; toss gently to combine. Divide salad
among serving bowls, sprinkle with nuts.
chilli citrus dressing place ingredients in screw-top jar; shake well.

preparation time 20 minutes (plus standing time) **serves** 4
nutritional count per serving 15.5g total fat (7.3g saturated fat);
1049kJ (251 cal); 16.3g carbohydrate; 7.9g protein; 8.4g fibre
tip you can add cooked prawns or shredded chicken to this salad.

Cauliflower salad with lemon mayonnaise

200g button mushrooms, halved
1 clove garlic, crushed
2 tablespoons olive oil
1 tablespoon finely grated lemon rind
¼ cup (60ml) lemon juice
1 small cauliflower (1kg), trimmed, cut into florets
1 cup (300g) mayonnaise
1 teaspoon water
1 medium red onion (170g), sliced thinly
150g baby spinach leaves

1 Combine mushrooms, garlic, oil, half the rind and two-thirds of the juice
in small bowl, cover; refrigerate 1 hour.
2 Meanwhile, boil, steam or microwave cauliflower until just tender; drain.
Rinse under cold water; drain.
3 Combine remaining rind, remaining juice, mayonnaise and the water
in small bowl.
4 Just before serving, combine mushrooms, cauliflower, onion and
spinach in large bowl; drizzle with lemon mayonnaise.

preparation time 15 minutes (plus refrigeration time)
cooking time 10 minutes   **serves** 4
nutritional count per serving 34.1g total fat (4g saturated fat);
1856kJ (444 cal); 22.8g carbohydrate; 9g protein; 7.4g fibre

Salami, bocconcini and pasta salad

500g mini penne pasta
½ cup (75g) seeded black olives, halved
250g cherry tomatoes, halved
180g bocconcini cheese, halved
100g spicy salami, chopped coarsely
1 cup firmly packed fresh basil leaves
red wine vinaigrette
⅓ cup (80ml) olive oil
¼ cup (60ml) red wine vinegar
2 teaspoons dijon mustard
1 clove garlic, crushed

1 Cook pasta in large saucepan of boiling water until just tender; drain. Rinse under cold water; drain.
2 Meanwhile, make red wine vinaigrette.
3 Place pasta in large bowl with remaining salad ingredients and dressing; toss gently to combine.
red wine vinaigrette place ingredients in screw-top jar; shake well.

preparation time 10 minutes **cooking time** 15 minutes **serves** 6
nutritional count per serving 24.1g total fat (4.9g saturated fat); 2274kJ (544 cal); 61g carbohydrate; 18.6g protein; 3.9g fibre

Rainbow salad

600g baby beetroot, trimmed
300g asparagus, trimmed
2 cloves garlic, crushed
1 tablespoon finely grated lemon rind
2 small avocados (400g), cut into thin wedges
3 medium oranges (720g), segmented
1 medium red onion (170g), sliced thinly
wholegrain mustard dressing
1 tablespoon wholegrain mustard
1 tablespoon cider vinegar
1 tablespoon finely chopped fresh chives
¼ cup coarsely chopped fresh flat-leaf parsley

1 Preheat oven to 180°C/160°C fan-forced.
2 Place beetroot on oven tray; roast uncovered, about 45 minutes or until beetroot is tender. Cool 10 minutes. Peel beetroot; cut in quarters.
3 Meanwhile, combine asparagus, garlic and rind on oven tray; roast, uncovered, about 10 minutes or until asparagus is tender. Cut asparagus in half, crossways.
4 Make wholegrain mustard dressing.
5 Place beetroot and asparagus mixture in large bowl with remaining ingredients and dressing; toss gently to combine.
wholegrain mustard dressing combine ingredients in small bowl.

preparation time 15 minutes **cooking time** 45 minutes **serves** 4
nutritional count per serving 16.3g total fat (3.4g saturated fat); 1166kJ (279 cal); 25.3g carbohydrate; 8g protein; 10.1g fibre

Chickpea and kumara salad

1 cup (200g) dried chickpeas
1 medium red onion (170g), chopped coarsely
1 medium red capsicum (200g), sliced thickly
1 medium kumara (400g), cut into 1cm pieces
2 cloves garlic, unpeeled
⅓ cup (80ml) olive oil
¼ cup (60ml) lemon juice
1 teaspoon english mustard
150g baby spinach leaves

1 Place chickpeas in medium bowl, cover with cold water; stand overnight, drain. Rinse under cold water; drain.
2 Preheat oven to 220°C/200°C fan-forced.
3 Place chickpeas in medium saucepan of boiling water; return to the boil. Reduce heat; simmer, uncovered, about 1 hour or until chickpeas are tender. Drain.
4 Meanwhile, toss onion, capsicum, kumara, garlic and 1 tablespoon of the oil in shallow baking dish. Roast about 30 minutes or until kumara is tender. Cool 10 minutes; remove garlic from dish.
5 Using back of fork, crush peeled garlic in large bowl; whisk in remaining oil, juice and mustard.
6 Add chickpeas, roasted vegetables and spinach to bowl; toss gently to combine.

preparation time 20 minutes (plus standing time)
cooking time 30 minutes   **serves 4**
nutritional count per serving 21.5g total fat (3g saturated fat);
1685kJ (403 cal); 34.9g carbohydrate; 12.7g protein; 10.3g fibre

stir-fries

Kung pao prawns

28 uncooked large prawns (2kg)
2 tablespoons peanut oil
2 cloves garlic, crushed
4 fresh small red thai chillies, chopped finely
1 teaspoon sichuan peppercorns, crushed
500g choy sum, trimmed, chopped coarsely
¼ cup (60ml) light soy sauce
¼ cup (60ml) chinese cooking wine
1 teaspoon white sugar
227g can water chestnuts, rinsed, halved
4 green onions, chopped coarsely
½ cup (70g) roasted unsalted peanuts

1 Shell and devein prawns, leaving tails intact.
2 Heat half the oil in wok; stir-fry prawns, in batches, until changed in colour. Drain.
3 Heat remaining oil in wok; stir-fry garlic, chilli and peppercorns until fragrant. Add choy sum; stir-fry until wilted.
4 Return prawns to wok with sauce, wine, sugar and chestnuts; stir-fry 2 minutes. Remove from heat; stir in onion and nuts.

preparation time 30 minutes **cooking time** 15 minutes **serves** 4
nutritional count per serving 19.4g total fat (2.9g saturated fat); 1998kJ (478 cal); 8.5g carbohydrate; 8.5g protein; 7.5g fibre
tip kung pao, a classic Sichuan stir-fry, is made with either seafood or chicken, peanuts and lots of chillies.

Mussels with kaffir lime and thai basil

1.5kg small black mussels
1 tablespoon peanut oil
3cm piece fresh ginger (15g), sliced thinly
1 clove garlic, sliced thinly
2 shallots (50g), sliced thinly
2 fresh long red chillies, sliced thinly
½ teaspoon ground turmeric
¼ cup (60ml) kecap manis
¼ cup (60ml) fish stock
¼ cup (60ml) water
2 tablespoons lime juice
2 fresh kaffir lime leaves, shredded finely
½ cup firmly packed fresh coriander leaves
½ cup firmly packed thai basil leaves

1 Scrub mussels under cold water; remove beards.
2 Heat oil in wok; stir-fry ginger, garlic, shallot, chilli and turmeric
until fragrant. Add kecap manis, stock and the water; bring to the boil.
Add mussels; simmer, covered, about 5 minutes or until mussels open
(discard any that do not).
3 Remove from heat, add remaining ingredients; toss gently to combine.

preparation time 30 minutes **cooking time** 10 minutes **serves** 4
nutritional count per serving 5.6g total fat (1.1g saturated fat);
414kJ (99 cal); 3.9g carbohydrate; 7.5g protein; 0.7g fibre

Prawn, scallop and lime stir-fry

500g uncooked large prawns
1 tablespoon sesame oil
2 cloves garlic, crushed
2cm piece fresh ginger (10g), grated
1 fresh small red thai chilli, sliced thinly
250g broccolini, chopped coarsely
200g asparagus, chopped coarsely
300g scallops
2 tablespoons lime juice
2 tablespoons soy sauce
4 green onions, sliced thinly

1 Shell and devein prawns, leaving tails intact.
2 Heat oil in wok; stir-fry garlic, ginger and chilli until fragrant. Add broccolini and asparagus; stir-fry until just tender.
3 Add prawns and scallops to wok; stir-fry until just cooked through. Add remaining ingredients; stir-fry until hot.

preparation time 15 minutes **cooking time** 15 minutes **serves** 4
nutritional count per serving 5.8g total fat (0.9g saturated fat); 744kJ (178 cal); 2.7g carbohydrate; 26.7g protein; 3.9g fibre
tip you can use gai lan or broccoli if broccolini is not available.

Garlic and chilli seafood stir-fry

720g uncooked medium prawns
2 cleaned squid hoods (300g)
540g octopus, quartered
¼ cup (60ml) peanut oil
6 cloves garlic, sliced thinly
2cm piece fresh ginger (10g), sliced thinly
2 fresh long red chillies, sliced thinly
2 tablespoons chinese cooking wine
1 teaspoon caster sugar
4 green onions, cut in 4cm pieces
chilli fried shallots
1 tablespoon fried shallots
1 teaspoon sea salt flakes
½ teaspoon dried chilli flakes

1 Shell and devein prawns, leaving tails intact. Cut squid down centre to open out; score inside in diagonal pattern then cut into thick strips. Quarter octopus lengthways.
2 Make chilli fried shallots.
3 Heat 1 tablespoon of the oil in wok; stir-fry prawns until changed in colour, remove from wok. Heat another tablespoon of the oil in wok; stir-fry squid until cooked through, remove from wok. Heat remaining oil in wok; stir-fry octopus until tender, remove from wok.
4 Stir-fry garlic, ginger and chilli in wok until fragrant. Return seafood to wok with remaining ingredients; stir-fry until hot.
5 Serve stir-fry sprinkled with chilli shallots.
chilli fried shallots combine ingredients in small bowl.

preparation time 25 minutes **cooking time** 20 minutes **serves** 4
nutritional count per serving 4.7g total fat (0.8g saturated fat);
460kJ (110 cal); 0.8g carbohydrate; 15.5g protein; 0.3g fibre

203

Tamarind honey prawns with pineapple

1.2kg uncooked medium king prawns
1 tablespoon vegetable oil
3 cloves garlic, crushed
1 fresh long red chilli, sliced thinly
1 medium red capsicum (200g), sliced thinly
150g snow peas, trimmed
⅓ cup (100g) tamarind concentrate
2 tablespoons kecap manis
1 tablespoon honey
230g can bamboo shoots, rinsed, drained
½ small pineapple (450g), chopped coarsely
4 green onions, sliced thinly

1 Shell and devein prawns, leaving tails intact.
2 Heat oil in wok; stir-fry prawns, garlic, chilli, capsicum and peas until prawns are changed in colour.
3 Add remaining ingredients to wok; stir-fry until hot.

preparation time 20 minutes **cooking time** 15 minutes **serves** 4
nutritional count per serving 5.8g total fat (0.8g saturated fat);
1141kJ (273 cal); 18.5g carbohydrate; 34.6g protein; 4.3g fibre

Prawn and scallop chilli jam stir-fry

1kg uncooked medium king prawns
2 tablespoons peanut oil
300g scallops, roe removed
2 cloves garlic, crushed
2cm piece fresh ginger (10g), grated
200g green beans, cut into 5cm lengths
350g gai lan, trimmed, chopped coarsely
⅔ cup (190g) prepared thai chilli jam
1½ cups (120g) bean sprouts
½ cup firmly packed thai basil leaves

1 Shell and devein prawns leaving tails intact.
2 Heat half the oil in wok; stir-fry prawns and scallops, in batches, until cooked as desired. Drain on absorbent paper.
3 Heat remaining oil in wok; stir-fry garlic and ginger until fragrant. Add beans and gai lan; stir-fry until gai lan is wilted. Return prawns and scallops to wok with chilli jam; stir-fry 2 minutes.
4 Stir in sprouts and basil off the heat; serve with steamed jasmine rice, if you like.

preparation time 20 minutes **cooking time** 20 minutes **serves** 4
nutritional count per serving 14.6g total fat (2.9g saturated fat);
1513kJ (362 cal); 16.8g carbohydrate; 38.6g protein; 3.9g fibre

Spiced coconut prawn stir-fry

1.25kg uncooked medium king prawns
500g cauliflower, cut into florets
200g broccoli, cut into florets
1 medium brown onion (150g), sliced thinly
2 cloves garlic, sliced thinly
2 fresh long red chillies, sliced thinly
1 teaspoon ground turmeric
2 teaspoons yellow mustard seeds
¼ teaspoon ground cardamom
½ teaspoon ground cumin
140ml can coconut milk
2 tablespoons mango chutney

1 Shell and devein prawns, leaving tails intact. Combine prawns and remaining ingredients in large bowl.
2 Stir-fry ingredients in heated oiled wok until prawns are cooked and vegetables are just tender.

preparation time 10 minutes **cooking time** 10 minutes **serves** 4
nutritional count per serving 8.7g total fat (6.5g saturated fat); 1225kJ (293 cal); 11.9g carbohydrate; 38.5g protein; 6g fibre

Prawn, asparagus and sesame stir-fry

1kg uncooked large king prawns
1 tablespoon peanut oil
5cm piece fresh ginger (25g), grated
2 cloves garlic, crushed
1 medium brown onion (150g), sliced thinly
300g asparagus, trimmed, chopped coarsely
1 fresh long red chilli, sliced thinly
2 tablespoons rice wine
¼ cup (60ml) soy sauce
2 teaspoons sesame oil
2 teaspoons brown sugar
2 teaspoons toasted sesame seeds

1 Shell and devein prawns, leaving tails intact.
2 Heat half the peanut oil in wok; stir-fry ginger, garlic and onion until fragrant. Add asparagus; stir-fry until tender. Remove from wok.
3 Heat remaining peanut oil in same wok; cook prawns, in batches, until cooked through.
4 Return prawns to wok with asparagus mixture, chilli and combined wine, sauce, sesame oil and sugar; stir-fry until mixture is heated through. Serve stir-fry sprinkled with seeds.

preparation time 30 minutes **cooking time** 15 minutes **serves** 4
nutritional count per serving 8.5g total fat (1.4g saturated fat);
907kJ (217 cal); 4.7g carbohydrate; 28.7g protein; 1.8g fibre

Mussels in black bean sauce

2kg medium black mussels
1 tablespoon peanut oil
6cm piece fresh ginger (30g), sliced thinly
4 cloves garlic, sliced thinly
8 green onions, sliced thinly
4 fresh small red thai chillies, chopped finely
⅓ cup (100g) black bean sauce
¼ cup (60ml) fish stock
¼ cup (60ml) water
1 cup firmly packed fresh coriander leaves

1 Scrub mussels under cold water; remove beards.
2 Heat oil in wok; stir-fry ginger, garlic, onion and chilli until fragrant.
Add sauce, stock and the water; bring to the boil.
3 Add mussels; simmer, covered, about 5 minutes or until mussels open
(discard any that do not). Remove from heat; sprinkle with coriander.

preparation time 10 minutes **cooking time** 10 minutes **serves** 4
nutritional count per serving 8.4g total fat (1g saturated fat);
882kJ (211 cal); 9.4g carbohydrate; 23.2g protein; 2.1g fibre

Fish and scallop stir-fry

2 tablespoons peanut oil
350g white fish steak, cut into strips
300g scallops, without roe
2 cloves garlic, crushed
4cm piece fresh ginger (20g), grated
2 medium carrots (240g), cut into matchsticks
2 shallots (50g), sliced thinly
227g can water chestnuts, rinsed, halved
1 small red capsicum (150g), sliced thinly
2 tablespoons water
1 tablespoon oyster sauce
1 tablespoon light soy sauce
1 tablespoon sweet chilli sauce
2 teaspoons golden syrup
150g snow peas, trimmed, sliced diagonally

1 Heat half the oil in wok; stir-fry fish until browned. Remove from wok.
2 Add scallops, garlic and ginger to wok; stir-fry until scallops change in colour. Remove from wok.
3 Heat remaining oil in wok; stir-fry carrot and shallot until browned. Add chestnuts, capsicum, the water, sauces and syrup; stir-fry until mixture thickens slightly.
4 Return seafood to wok with snow peas; stir-fry until just tender.

preparation time 20 minutes **cooking time** 10 minutes **serves** 4
nutritional count per serving 12.3g total fat (2.5g saturated fat);
1258kJ (301 cal); 15.6g carbohydrate; 29.7g protein; 4.6g fibre
tip we used swordfish in this recipe, but you can use any firm white fish.

Chilli, salt and pepper seafood

500g uncooked medium king prawns
300g cleaned squid hoods
300g scallops, roe removed
2 teaspoons sea salt
½ teaspoon cracked black pepper
½ teaspoon five-spice powder
2 fresh small red thai chillies, chopped finely
2 tablespoons peanut oil
150g sugar snap peas, trimmed
2 tablespoons light soy sauce
1 lime, cut into wedges

1 Shell and devein prawns, leaving tails intact. Cut squid down centre to open out; score inside in diagonal pattern then cut into thick strips.
2 Combine seafood, salt, pepper, five-spice and chilli in large bowl.
3 Heat half the oil in wok; stir-fry seafood, in batches, until cooked.
4 Heat remaining oil in wok; stir-fry peas until tender. Return seafood to wok with sauce; stir-fry until hot. Serve seafood with lime.

preparation time 15 minutes **cooking time** 15 minutes **serves** 4
nutritional count per serving 11g total fat (2.2g saturated fat);
1070kJ (256 cal); 2.7g carbohydrate; 35.8g protein; 1.2g fibre

Chicken, mixed vegies and almond stir-fry

2½ cups (500g) jasmine rice
2 tablespoons peanut oil
600g chicken breast fillets, sliced thinly
1 medium brown onion (150g), sliced thinly
2 cloves garlic, crushed
350g broccolini, trimmed, chopped coarsely
115g fresh baby corn, halved lengthways
150g sugar snap peas, trimmed
⅓ cup (45g) roasted slivered almonds
1 tablespoon fish sauce
1 tablespoon sweet chilli sauce

1 Cook rice in large saucepan of boiling water until just tender; drain. Cover to keep warm.
2 Meanwhile, heat half the oil in wok; stir-fry chicken, in batches, until browned lightly and cooked through.
3 Heat remaining oil in wok; stir-fry onion and garlic until onion softens. Add broccolini, corn and peas; stir-fry until vegetables are tender.
4 Return chicken to wok with nuts and sauces; stir-fry until heated through. Serve with rice.

preparation time 15 minutes **cooking time** 20 minutes **serves** 4
nutritional count per serving 20.2g total fat (3.1g saturated fat);
3515kJ (841 cal); 109.4g carbohydrate; 50.5g protein; 7.5g fibre

Capsicum, chilli and hoisin chicken

800g chicken breast fillets, sliced thinly
10cm stick fresh lemon grass (20g), chopped finely
2cm piece fresh ginger (10g), grated
2 cloves garlic, crushed
1½ teaspoons five-spice powder
2 tablespoons peanut oil
1 medium brown onion (150g), sliced thinly
1 fresh long red chilli, chopped finely
1 medium red capsicum (200g), sliced thickly
⅓ cup (80ml) hoisin sauce
2 teaspoons finely grated lemon rind
1 tablespoon lemon juice
½ cup coarsely chopped fresh coriander
2 tablespoons fried shallots
1 green onion, sliced thinly

1 Combine chicken with lemon grass, ginger, half the garlic and
1 teaspoon of the five-spice in large bowl. Cover; refrigerate 1 hour.
2 Heat half the oil in wok; stir-fry brown onion, chilli, capsicum and
remaining garlic, until onion softens. Remove from wok.
3 Heat remaining oil in wok; stir-fry chicken, in batches, until cooked.
4 Return onion mixture and chicken to wok with sauce, rind, juice and
remaining five-spice; stir-fry until sauce thickens slightly. Remove from
heat; toss coriander into stir-fry, sprinkle with shallots and green onion.

preparation time 15 minutes (plus refrigeration time)
cooking time 15 minutes **serves** 4
nutritional count per serving 15.4g total fat (3.1g saturated fat);
1601kJ (383 cal); 12.1g carbohydrate; 47.2g protein; 3.9g fibre

Thai basil chicken and snake bean stir-fry

800g chicken thigh fillets, sliced thinly
¼ cup (60ml) fish sauce
1 tablespoon grated palm sugar
¼ teaspoon ground white pepper
1 tablespoon peanut oil
3 cloves garlic, sliced thinly
2cm piece fresh ginger (10g), sliced thinly
½ teaspoon dried chilli flakes
250g snake beans, cut into 5cm lengths
2 medium yellow capsicums (400g), sliced thinly
⅓ cup (80ml) chinese cooking wine
⅓ cup (80ml) lemon juice
1 tablespoon dark soy sauce
½ cup loosely packed thai basil leaves

1 Combine chicken, fish sauce, sugar and pepper in large bowl.
Cover; refrigerate 1 hour.
2 Heat oil in wok; stir-fry chicken mixture, in batches, until almost cooked.
3 Return chicken to wok, add garlic, ginger, chilli, beans and capsicum;
stir-fry until beans are tender.
4 Add wine, juice and soy sauce to wok; bring to the boil. Reduce heat;
simmer, uncovered, 2 minutes. Remove from heat; stir in basil.

preparation time 20 minutes (plus refrigeration time)
cooking time 20 minutes **serves** 4
nutritional count per serving 19.4g total fat (5.2g saturated fat);
1622kJ (388 cal); 8.6g carbohydrate; 42.4g protein; 3.3g fibre

Chengdu chicken

2 tablespoons light soy sauce
2 tablespoons chinese cooking wine
1 teaspoon sesame oil
800g chicken breast fillets, chopped coarsely
¼ cup (60ml) peanut oil
300g spinach, trimmed, chopped coarsely
2 cloves garlic, crushed
2cm piece fresh ginger (10g), grated
4 green onions, sliced thinly
1 tablespoon rice vinegar
1 teaspoon white sugar
2 tablespoons finely grated orange rind
2 tablespoons sambal oelek
1 teaspoon sichuan peppercorns, crushed

1 Combine half the sauce, half the wine and half the sesame oil in large bowl with chicken. Cover; refrigerate 20 minutes.
2 Heat 1 tablespoon of the peanut oil in wok; stir-fry spinach until just wilted. Remove from wok; cover to keep warm.
3 Heat half the remaining peanut oil in wok; stir-fry chicken mixture, in batches, until browned. Heat remaining peanut oil in wok; stir-fry garlic, ginger and onion until onion just softens.
4 Return chicken and remaining sauce, wine and sesame oil to wok with vinegar, sugar, rind and sambal; stir-fry until chicken is cooked.
5 Serve spinach topped with chicken; sprinkle with pepper.

preparation time 20 minutes (plus refrigeration time)
cooking time 15 minutes **serves** 4
nutritional count per serving 19.8g total fat (3.8g saturated fat); 1710kJ (409 cal); 5.7g carbohydrate; 48g protein; 2.1g fibre

Chicken and yellow bean relish

3 cloves garlic, quartered
2 purple shallots (50g), chopped coarsely
1 tablespoon vegetable oil
2 tablespoons yellow bean paste
150g chicken mince
$\frac{1}{3}$ cup (80ml) coconut cream
2 tablespoons chicken stock
$\frac{1}{4}$ teaspoon dried chilli flakes
$\frac{1}{3}$ cup loosely packed fresh coriander leaves
$\frac{1}{3}$ cup coarsely chopped fresh mint
8 large trimmed wombok leaves

1 Using mortar and pestle, crush garlic and shallot until it forms a paste.
2 Heat oil in wok; stir-fry garlic mixture until browned lightly. Add paste; stir-fry until fragrant.
3 Add chicken to wok; stir-fry until cooked through. Add coconut cream, stock and chilli; bring to the boil. Reduce heat; simmer, uncovered, about 5 minutes or until thickened. Remove from heat; stir in herbs.
4 Serve relish with wombok leaves, sliced cucumber and carrot sticks, if you like.

preparation time 10 minutes **cooking time** 10 minutes **makes** 1 cup
nutritional count per tablespoon 4.1g total fat (1.7g saturated); 238kJ (57 cal); 1.4g carbohydrate; 3.4g protein; 1g fibre
tip due to the richness of this relish, you only need to serve a small amount to enjoy its delicious flavour.

Chilli chicken with broccoli and cashews

1 tablespoon peanut oil
600g chicken mince
1 clove garlic, crushed
1 small brown onion (80g), sliced thinly
300g broccoli, cut into florets
2 tablespoons fish sauce
1 tablespoon hot chilli sauce
8 green onions, sliced thinly
1¼ cups (100g) bean sprouts
⅓ cup (50g) roasted unsalted cashews
4 kaffir lime leaves, sliced thinly
1 fresh long red chilli, sliced thinly

1 Heat half the oil in wok; stir-fry chicken, in batches, until cooked.
2 Heat remaining oil in wok; stir-fry garlic and brown onion until onion softens. Add broccoli; stir-fry until almost tender.
3 Return chicken to wok with sauces, green onion, sprouts, nuts and leaves; stir-fry just until hot. Remove from heat; sprinkle with chilli.

preparation time 10 minutes **cooking time** 20 minutes **serves** 4
nutritional count per serving 23.4g total fat (5.6g saturated fat); 1643kJ (393 cal); 6.3g carbohydrate; 36.9g protein; 5.8g fibre

Chilli orange duck and mango

2 medium mangoes (860g), peeled
1 tablespoon vegetable oil
750g duck breast fillets, skinned, sliced thinly
4cm piece fresh ginger (20g), grated
1 fresh small red thai chilli, chopped finely
175g broccolini, chopped coarsely
½ cup (125ml) orange juice
¼ cup (60ml) chicken stock
2 tablespoons sweet chilli sauce
4 green onions, sliced thinly
⅓ cup (50g) roasted unsalted cashews
1 tablespoon finely chopped fresh mint

1 Slice cheeks from mangoes; slice each cheek into matchsticks.
2 Heat oil in wok; stir-fry duck, in batches, until just browned.
3 Stir-fry ginger and chilli until fragrant. Add broccolini; stir-fry until just tender. Add juice, stock and sauce; bring to the boil. Cook until sauce thickens slightly.
4 Return duck to wok with mango and onion; stir-fry until duck is hot. Remove from heat; serve sprinkled with nuts and mint.

preparation time 15 minutes **cooking time** 15 minutes **serves** 4
nutritional count per serving 21.9g total fat (4.8g saturated fat);
1990kJ (476 cal); 27.2g carbohydrate; 39.9g protein; 5.9g fibre

231

Twice-fried sichuan beef with buk choy

½ cup (75g) cornflour
1 tablespoon sichuan peppercorns, crushed coarsely
600g piece beef eye fillet, sliced thinly
vegetable oil, for deep-frying
2 teaspoons sesame oil
1 clove garlic, crushed
2 fresh small red thai chillies, chopped finely
1 medium brown onion (150g), sliced thinly
1 medium carrot (120g), halved, sliced thinly
1 medium red capsicum (200g), sliced thinly
150g sugar snap peas, trimmed
300g baby buk choy, leaves separated
2 tablespoons oyster sauce
¼ cup (60ml) japanese soy sauce
¼ cup (60ml) beef stock
2 tablespoons dry sherry
1 tablespoon brown sugar

1 Combine cornflour and half the pepper in medium bowl with beef.
2 Heat vegetable oil in wok; deep-fry beef, in batches, until crisp. Drain on absorbent paper.
3 Heat sesame oil in cleaned wok; stir-fry garlic, chilli and onion until onion softens. Add carrot and capsicum; stir-fry until vegetables soften.
4 Return beef to wok with remaining ingredients; stir-fry until buk choy is wilted.

preparation time 20 minutes **cooking time** 25 minutes **serves** 4
nutritional count per serving 19.5g total fat (5.1g saturated fat);
1914kJ (458cal); 29.6g carbohydrate; 36.4g protein; 3.8g fibre

Chilli-garlic mince with snake beans

2 cloves garlic, quartered
2 long green chillies, chopped coarsely
2 fresh small red thai chillies, chopped coarsely
1 tablespoon peanut oil
600g beef mince
150g snake beans, chopped coarsely
1 medium red capsicum (200g), sliced thinly
2 tablespoons kecap asin
¼ cup (60ml) hoisin sauce
4 green onions, sliced thickly
2 tablespoons crushed peanuts

1 Blend or process garlic and chilli until mixture is finely chopped.
2 Heat half the oil in wok; stir-fry garlic mixture until fragrant. Add beef; stir-fry, in batches, until cooked through.
3 Heat remaining oil in cleaned wok; stir-fry beans and capsicum until tender.
4 Return beef to wok with sauces and onion; stir-fry until hot. Sprinkle with nuts; serve with lime wedges, if you like.

preparation time 10 minutes **cooking time** 15 minutes **serves** 4
nutritional count per serving 18.6g total fat (5.6g saturated fat);
1476kJ (353 cal); 9.6g carbohydrate; 34.8g protein; 4.2g fibre
tip kecap asin is a thick, dark, salty soy sauce, available from Asian food shops and some supermarkets.

Spinach and beef stir-fry

2 tablespoons peanut oil
700g beef strips
2 cloves garlic, crushed
250g broccolini, chopped coarsely
300g enoki mushrooms
250g baby spinach leaves
¼ cup (60ml) beef stock
¼ cup (60ml) oyster sauce

1 Heat half the oil in wok; stir-fry beef, in batches, until browned all over.
2 Heat remaining oil in same wok; stir-fry garlic and broccolini until just tender.
3 Return beef to wok with remaining ingredients; stir-fry until spinach is just wilted.

preparation time 10 minutes **cooking time** 20 minutes **serves** 4
nutritional count per serving 25.9g total fat (8.9g saturated fat); 1848kJ (442 cal); 5.1g carbohydrate; 44.3g protein; 6.4g fibre

Beef in satay sauce

1 tablespoon peanut oil
750g beef strips
1 fresh long red chilli, sliced thinly
1 medium brown onion (150g), sliced thinly
1 medium red capsicum (200g),sliced thinly
½ cup (140g) peanut butter
½ cup (125ml) coconut cream
¼ cup (60ml) sweet chilli sauce
1 tablespoon japanese soy sauce

1 Heat half the oil in wok; stir-fry beef, in batches, until cooked.
2 Heat remaining oil in wok; stir-fry chilli, onion and capsicum until soft.
Remove from wok.
3 Combine peanut butter, coconut cream and sauces in wok; bring to
the boil. Return beef and onion mixture to wok; stir-fry until hot.

preparation time 10 minutes **cooking time** 20 minutes **serves** 4
nutritional count per serving 42.2g total fat (15g saturated fat);
2629kJ (629 cal); 10.6g carbohydrate; 49.8g protein; 6.1g fibre

Pepper beef and mushroom stir-fry

700g beef strips
2 teaspoons cracked black pepper
2 teaspoons ground sichuan pepper
2 tablespoons vegetable oil
1 medium brown onion (150g), sliced thickly
2 cloves garlic, crushed
100g shiitake mushrooms, halved
100g oyster mushrooms, halved
200g button mushrooms, halved
2 teaspoons cornflour
1 tablespoon water
⅓ cup (80ml) mirin
¼ cup (60ml) soy sauce

1 Combine beef and peppers in medium bowl.
2 Heat half the oil in wok; stir-fry beef, in batches, until browned all over.
3 Heat remaining oil in same wok; stir-fry onion and garlic until onion is just tender. Add mushrooms; stir-fry until mushrooms are just tender.
4 Add blended cornflour and water, then mirin and sauce; stir-fry until mixture boils and thickens slightly.
5 Return beef to wok; stir-fry until heated through.

preparation time 10 minutes **cooking time** 20 minutes **serves** 4
nutritional count per serving 22.1g total fat (5.9g saturated fat); 1676kJ (401 cal); 4.6g carbohydrate; 41.6g protein; 3.6g fibre
tip you can use dry sherry instead of mirin.

Chinese minced beef and spicy green beans

1 tablespoon peanut oil
800g beef mince
2 cloves garlic, crushed
3cm piece fresh ginger (15g), grated
2 long green chillies, sliced thinly lengthways
300g green beans, halved lengthways
1 medium brown onion (150g), sliced thinly
1 tablespoon lime juice
2 tablespoons light soy sauce
1 tablespoon white sugar
⅓ cup (45g) crushed roasted unsalted peanuts

1 Heat half the oil in wok; stir-fry beef, in batches, until browned and cooked.
2 Heat remaining oil in wok; stir-fry garlic, ginger, chilli, beans and onion until beans are almost tender.
3 Return beef to wok with juice, sauce and sugar; stir-fry until hot. Serve stir-fry sprinkled with nuts.

preparation time 10 minutes **cooking time** 15 minutes **serves** 4
nutritional count per serving 23.9g total fat (7.2g saturated fat); 1864kJ (446 cal); 9.7g carbohydrate; 46.3g protein; 3.8g fibre

Chilli jam beef

2 tablespoons vegetable oil
800g beef strips
1 medium brown onion (150g), chopped coarsely
2 cloves garlic, crushed
115g baby corn, halved lengthways
150g snow peas, halved crossways
½ cup (160g) chilli jam
2 teaspoons finely grated lime rind
2 tablespoons lime juice

1 Heat half the oil in wok; cook beef, in batches, until browned.
2 Heat remaining oil in wok; cook onion and garlic, stirring, until onion softens. Add corn; cook, stirring, until corn is just tender.
3 Return beef to wok with peas, jam, rind and juice; stir-fry until sauce thickens slightly.

preparation time 10 minutes **cooking time** 10 minutes **serves** 4
nutritional count per serving 24.7g total fat (7g saturated fat);
2057kJ (492 cal); 19.6g carbohydrate; 46.4g protein; 3g fibre

Peppercorn beef

2 tablespoons dark soy sauce
3cm piece fresh ginger (15g), grated
2 cloves garlic, crushed
2 teaspoons cornflour
1 teaspoon sesame oil
800g beef rump steak, sliced thinly
2 teaspoons pepper medley
¼ teaspoon sichuan peppercorns
2 tablespoons peanut oil
1 medium brown onion (150g), sliced thinly
150g snake beans, chopped coarsely
2 tablespoons chinese cooking wine
½ cup (125ml) water
2 tablespoons oyster sauce
4 green onions, sliced thickly

1 Combine soy sauce, ginger, garlic, cornflour and sesame oil in large bowl with beef. Cover; refrigerate 1 hour.
2 Meanwhile, using mortar and pestle, crush pepper medley and sichuan peppercorns finely.
3 Heat half the peanut oil in wok; stir-fry beef, in batches, until browned.
4 Heat remaining oil in wok; stir-fry brown onion, beans and pepper mixture until onion is tender.
5 Return beef to wok with wine, the water and oyster sauce; bring to the boil. Stir-fry until beans are cooked. Remove from heat; stir in green onion.

preparation time 20 minutes (plus refrigeration time)
cooking time 20 minutes **serves** 4
nutritional count per serving 24g total fat (7.8g saturated fat); 1889kJ (452 cal); 7.6g carbohydrate; 47.8g protein; 2.1g fibre
tip pepper medley is a mixture of black, white, green and pink peppercorns, coriander seeds and allspice, sold in grinders in supermarkets. You can use your own blend of various peppercorns, if you prefer.

Ginger teriyaki beef

⅓ cup (80ml) teriyaki sauce
½ cup (125ml) hoisin sauce
2 tablespoons mirin
1 tablespoon peanut oil
750g beef strips
250g broccoli, cut into florets
250g sugar snap peas, trimmed
115g fresh baby corn, halved lengthways
4cm piece fresh ginger (20g), grated
1½ cups (120g) bean sprouts

1 Combine sauces and mirin in small jug.
2 Heat half the oil in wok; stir-fry beef, in batches, until browned.
3 Heat remaining oil in wok; stir-fry broccoli until almost tender.
4 Return beef to wok with sauce mixture, peas, corn and ginger. Stir-fry until vegetables and beef are cooked. Remove from heat; sprinkle with sprouts.

preparation time 10 minutes **cooking time** 15 minutes **serves** 4
nutritional count per serving 20.7g total fat (7.2g saturated fat); 2073kJ (496 cal); 23.2g carbohydrate; 48g protein; 10.5g fibre

Beef and black bean stir-fry

2 tablespoons peanut oil
700g beef strips
200g green beans, cut into 5cm lengths
1 medium carrot (120g), sliced thinly
1 medium red capsicum (200g), sliced thinly
1 clove garlic, crushed
¼ cup (60ml) beef stock
¼ cup (60ml) black bean sauce
4 green onions, sliced thinly
230g can bamboo shoots, drained

1 Heat half the oil in wok; stir fry beef, in batches, until browned all over.
2 Heat remaining oil in same wok; stir-fry beans, carrot, capsicum and garlic until vegetables are just tender.
3 Return beef to wok with remaining ingredients; stir-fry until hot.

preparation time 10 minutes **cooking time** 10 minutes **serves** 4
nutritional count per serving 25.8g total fat (9g saturated fat);
1818kJ (435 cal); 9.1g carbohydrate; 39.9g protein; 4.1g fibre

251

Lemon veal stir-fry with capsicum and pecans

1 tablespoon peanut oil
600g veal steaks, sliced thinly
2 medium brown onions (300g), cut into thin wedges
1 medium red capsicum (200g), sliced thinly
1 medium green capsicum (200g), sliced thinly
2 tablespoons finely chopped fresh lemon grass
⅓ cup (35g) pecans, halved lengthways
2 teaspoons grated lemon rind
⅓ cup (80ml) lemon juice
⅓ cup (80ml) soy sauce
1 clove garlic, crushed

1 Heat oil in wok; stir-fry veal, in batches, until browned.
2 Add onion, capsicums and lemon grass to wok; stir-fry until vegetables are soft. Stir in nuts; cook 1 minute.
3 Return veal to wok with combined rind, juice, sauce and garlic; stir-fry until heated through.

preparation time 10 minutes **cooking time** 15 minutes **serves** 4
nutritional count per serving 16.3g total fat (2.7g saturated fat);
1404kJ (336 cal); 8.3g carbohydrate; 37.7g protein; 2.8g fibre

Stir-fried beef and mixed mushrooms

¼ cup (60ml) peanut oil
800g beef rump steak, sliced thinly
1 medium brown onion (150g), sliced thickly
2 cloves garlic, crushed
2cm piece fresh ginger (10g), grated
2 fresh long red chillies, sliced thinly
150g oyster mushrooms, halved
100g fresh shiitake mushrooms, halved
100g enoki mushrooms
450g hokkien noodles
6 green onions, sliced thickly
¼ cup (60ml) oyster sauce
1 tablespoon kecap manis
1 teaspoon sesame oil

1 Heat half the peanut oil in wok; stir-fry beef, in batches, until browned.
2 Heat remaining peanut oil in same wok; stir-fry onion until soft.
Add garlic, ginger, chilli and mushrooms; stir-fry until mushrooms are
just tender.
3 Meanwhile, place noodles in large heatproof bowl, cover with boiling
water, separate with fork; drain.
4 Return beef to wok with noodles and remaining ingredients; stir-fry
until mixture boils and thickens slightly.

preparation time 15 minutes **cooking time** 15 minutes **serves** 4
nutritional count per serving 29.9g total fat (8.9g saturated fat);
3298kJ (789 cal); 70.1g carbohydrate; 59.2g protein; 6.6g fibre

Aromatic beef stir-fry

2 tablespoons peanut oil
800g beef strips
1 medium brown onion (150g), chopped finely
3 cloves garlic, crushed
1 fresh long red chilli, chopped finely
10cm stick fresh lemon grass (20g), chopped finely
1 star anise
1 cinnamon stick
4 cardamom pods, bruised
350g snake beans, cut in 4cm lengths
2 tablespoons ground bean sauce
2 tablespoons fish sauce
½ cup coarsely chopped fresh coriander
½ cup (40g) roasted almond flakes

1 Heat half the oil in wok; stir-fry beef, in batches, until browned.
2 Heat remaining oil in wok; stir-fry onion until soft. Add garlic, chilli, lemon grass, star anise, cinnamon, cardamom and beans; stir-fry until beans are tender. Discard star anise, cinnamon and cardamom.
3 Return beef to wok with sauces; stir-fry until heated through. Stir in coriander and nuts off the heat.

preparation time 15 minutes **cooking time** 15 minutes **serves** 4
nutritional count per serving 27.2g total fat (7.2g saturated fat); 2002kJ (479 cal); 7.3g carbohydrate; 49.5g protein; 4.8g fibre
tip ground bean sauce is a mixture of soy beans, flour, salt, sugar and water. To make your own version of ground bean sauce, add 1 teaspoon white sugar to 1 tablespoon black bean sauce.

Crisp beef with gai lan

2 tablespoons cornflour
½ teaspoon bicarbonate of soda
500g beef strips
½ cup (125ml) peanut oil
¼ cup (60ml) sweet chilli sauce
2 tablespoons soy sauce
1 clove garlic, crushed
1 teaspoon sesame oil
1 large red onion (300g), sliced thinly
½ small wombok (400g), shredded coarsely
400g gai lan, chopped coarsely

1 Combine cornflour and soda in large bowl. Add beef; toss to coat all over, shaking off excess.
2 Heat one-third of the peanut oil in wok; stir-fry about a third of the beef until crisp. Drain on absorbent paper; cover to keep warm. Repeat with remaining peanut oil and beef.
3 Combine sauces and garlic in small bowl.
4 Heat sesame oil in cleaned wok; stir-fry onion until just tender. Add wombok and gai lan; stir-fry 1 minute. Add sauce mixture and beef; stir-fry until heated through.

preparation time 15 minutes **cooking time** 15 minutes **serves** 4
nutritional count per serving 41.7g total fat (10.5g saturated fat);
2320kJ (555 cal); 13.8g carbohydrate; 30g protein; 4.4g fibre

Beef kway teow

¼ cup (60ml) oyster sauce
2 tablespoons kecap manis
2 tablespoons chinese cooking wine
1 teaspoon sambal oelek
3 cloves garlic, crushed
2cm piece fresh ginger (10g), grated
2 tablespoons peanut oil
500g beef strips
450g fresh wide rice noodles
6 green onions, cut into 2cm lengths
1 small red capsicum (150g), sliced thinly
1 small green capsicum (150g), sliced thinly
¼ cup coarsely chopped garlic chives
2 cups (160g) bean sprouts

1 Combine sauces, wine, sambal, garlic and ginger in small jug.
2 Heat half the oil in wok; stir-fry beef, in batches, until browned lightly.
3 Place noodles in large heatproof bowl, cover with boiling water; separate with fork, drain.
4 Heat remaining oil in wok; stir-fry onion and capsicums until tender.
5 Return beef to wok with sauce mixture, noodles, chives and sprouts; stir-fry until hot.

preparation time 10 minutes **cooking time** 10 minutes **serves** 4
nutritional count per serving 17.7g total fat (4.8g saturated fat); 2195kJ (525 cal); 53g carbohydrate; 34.4g protein; 3.8g fibre

Lemon veal with asian greens

2 tablespoons vegetable oil
750g veal strips
10cm stick fresh lemon grass (20g), chopped finely
500g baby buk choy, trimmed, quartered lengthways
500g choy sum, trimmed, halved crossways
2 cloves garlic, crushed
2 teaspoons finely grated lemon rind
¼ cup (60ml) lemon juice
¼ cup (60ml) dark soy sauce
4 green onions, sliced thinly
⅓ cup (55g) roasted almonds, chopped coarsely

1 Heat half the oil in wok; stir-fry veal, in batches, until browned.
2 Heat remaining oil in wok; stir-fry lemon grass until fragrant. Add buk choy, choy sum, garlic, rind, juice and sauce; stir-fry until vegetables are wilted.
3 Return veal to wok with onion; stir-fry until hot. Remove from heat; sprinkle with nuts.

preparation time 10 minutes **cooking time** 15 minutes **serves** 4
nutritional count per serving 20.2g total fat (2.4g saturated fat);
1705kJ (408 cal); 4.6g carbohydrate; 48.6g protein; 5.1g fibre

Stir-fried lamb in hoisin sauce

2 tablespoons peanut oil
600g lamb strips
2 cloves garlic, crushed
2cm piece fresh ginger (10g), grated
1 medium brown onion (150g), sliced thinly
1 small red capsicum (150g), sliced thinly
1 small yellow capsicum (150g), sliced thinly
6 green onions, sliced thinly
⅓ cup (80ml) chicken stock
1 tablespoon soy sauce
¼ cup (60ml) hoisin sauce

1 Heat half the oil in wok; stir-fry lamb, in batches, until browned all over.
2 Heat remaining oil in same wok; stir-fry garlic, ginger and brown onion until onion is just tender. Add capsicums and green onion; stir-fry until capsicum is just tender.
3 Return lamb to wok, add combined stock and sauces; stir until sauce boils and thickens slightly and lamb is cooked as desired.

preparation time 15 minutes **cooking time** 15 minutes **serves** 4
nutritional count per serving 24.5g total fat (7.8g saturated fat); 1672kJ (400 cal); 11.6g carbohydrate; 34.1g protein; 3.5g fibre

Lamb char siu stir-fry

2 tablespoons rice vinegar
2 tablespoons peanut oil
2 tablespoons char siu sauce
1 tablespoon kecap manis
2 cloves garlic, crushed
600g lamb fillets, sliced thickly
1 tablespoon peanut oil, extra
200g broccolini, trimmed
200g snow peas, trimmed
200g sugar snap peas, trimmed
1 fresh long red chilli, sliced thinly

1 Combine vinegar, oil, sauce, kecap manis, garlic and lamb in medium bowl. Drain lamb; reserve sauce mixture.
2 Cook lamb, in batches, in heated oiled wok until browned.
3 Heat extra oil in cleaned wok; stir-fry broccolini and peas, in batches.
4 Return vegetables and lamb to wok with reserved sauce mixture; stir-fry until hot. Serve sprinkled with chilli.

preparation time 15 minutes **cooking time** 20 minutes **serves** 4
nutritional count per serving 19.6g total fat (4.9g saturated fat);
1517kJ (363 cal); 7.9g carbohydrate; 36.8g protein; 4.6g fibre

Honey and five-spice lamb with buk choy

¼ teaspoon five-spice powder
¼ cup (60ml) oyster sauce
2 tablespoons honey
2 tablespoons rice vinegar
2 cloves garlic, crushed
600g lamb fillets, sliced thinly
400g fresh thin rice noodles
1 tablespoon sesame oil
2 fresh long red chillies, sliced thinly
2cm piece fresh ginger (10g), cut into matchsticks
1 medium red onion (150g), sliced thickly
500g baby buk choy, leaves separated
¼ cup firmly packed fresh coriander leaves
1 tablespoon crushed peanuts

1 Combine five-spice, sauce, honey, vinegar and garlic in small bowl.
2 Combine lamb with 1 tablespoon of the five-spice mixture in medium bowl.
3 Place noodles in large heatproof bowl, cover with boiling water; separate noodles with fork, drain.
4 Heat oil in wok; stir-fry lamb, in batches, until browned. Return to wok; add chilli, ginger, onion and remaining five-spice mixture; stir-fry until onion softens. Add noodles and buk choy; stir-fry until hot.
5 Serve stir-fry sprinkled with coriander and nuts.

preparation time 15 minutes **cooking time** 10 minutes **serves** 4
nutritional count per serving 12.2g total fat (3.3g saturated fat); 1781kJ (426 cal); 40.7g carbohydrate; 36.1g protein; 3.3g fibre

Hoisin sweet chilli lamb and mixed vegetables

1 tablespoon peanut oil
750g lamb strips
2 cloves garlic, sliced thinly
400g packaged fresh stir-fry vegetables
⅓ cup (80ml) hoisin sauce
2 tablespoons sweet chilli sauce
2 tablespoons water

1 Heat half the oil in wok; stir-fry lamb, in batches, until cooked.
2 Heat remaining oil in wok; stir-fry garlic and vegetables until vegetables are almost tender.
3 Return lamb to wok with sauces and the water; stir-fry until hot.

preparation time 10 minutes **cooking time** 15 minutes **serves** 4
nutritional count per serving 23.1g total fat (8.7g saturated fat); 1877kJ (449 cal); 17.2g carbohydrate; 41.4g protein; 4.5g fibre

Lamb teriyaki with broccolini

1 tablespoon vegetable oil
800g lamb strips
4 green onions, chopped coarsely
3cm piece fresh ginger (15g), grated
175g broccolini, chopped coarsely
150g green beans, trimmed, halved crossways
⅓ cup (80ml) teriyaki sauce
2 tablespoons honey
2 teaspoons sesame oil
1 tablespoon roasted sesame seeds

1 Heat half the vegetable oil in wok; stir-fry lamb, in batches, until browned all over.
2 Heat remaining vegetable oil in wok; stir-fry onion and ginger until onion softens. Add broccolini and beans; stir-fry until vegetables are tender. Remove from wok.
3 Add sauce, honey and sesame oil to wok; bring to the boil. Boil, uncovered, about 3 minutes or until sauce thickens slightly.
4 Return lamb and vegetables to wok; stir-fry until hot. Serve sprinkled with seeds.

preparation time 10 minutes **cooking time** 15 minutes **serves** 4
nutritional count per serving 15.9g total fat (4.3g saturated fat);
1626kJ (389 cal); 14.1g carbohydrate; 45.7g protein; 3.4g fibre

Hunan lamb

1 tablespoon chinese cooking wine
1 tablespoon light soy sauce
2cm piece fresh ginger (10g), grated
4 fresh small red thai chillies, chopped finely
1 clove garlic, crushed
800g lamb backstraps, sliced thinly
2 tablespoons peanut oil
2 large leeks (1kg), trimmed, sliced thinly
½ cup (125ml) chicken stock
2 tablespoons rice vinegar
2 tablespoons grated palm sugar
½ cup (70g) roasted unsalted pistachios
½ cup coarsely chopped fresh mint leaves

1 Combine wine, sauce, ginger, chilli, garlic and lamb in medium bowl.
2 Heat 1 tablespoon of the oil in wok; stir-fry lamb, in batches, until browned all over.
3 Heat remaining oil in cleaned wok; stir-fry leek until browned lightly. Add stock, vinegar and sugar; bring to the boil.
4 Return lamb to wok with nuts; stir-fry until lamb is cooked. Remove from heat; stir in mint.

preparation time 30 minutes **cooking time** 15 minutes **serves** 4
nutritional count per serving 35.8g total fat (10.7g saturated fat); 4500kJ (598 cal); 16g carbohydrate; 49.4g protein; 6.8g fibre
tip Hunan, a steamy, hot region in mountainous southwest China near Sichuan, has a cuisine that similarly teems with heat, its restaurants full of spicy foods just like this classic example.

Larb lamb

1 tablespoon peanut oil
5cm stick fresh lemon grass (10g), chopped finely
2 fresh small red thai chillies, chopped finely
2 cloves garlic, crushed
3cm piece fresh ginger (15g), chopped finely
750g lamb mince
1 lebanese cucumber (130g), seeded, sliced thinly
1 small red onion (100g), sliced thinly
1 cup (80g) bean sprouts
½ cup loosely packed thai basil leaves
1 cup loosely packed fresh coriander leaves
8 large iceberg lettuce leaves
dressing
⅓ cup (80ml) lime juice
2 tablespoons fish sauce
2 tablespoons kecap manis
2 tablespoons peanut oil
2 teaspoons grated palm sugar
½ teaspoon sambal oelek

1 Make dressing.
2 Heat oil in wok; stir-fry lemon grass, chilli, garlic and ginger until fragrant. Add lamb; stir-fry, in batches, until changed in colour.
3 Return lamb to wok with a third of the dressing; stir-fry about 2 minutes or until most of the liquid has evaporated.
4 Place lamb mixture in large bowl with cucumber, onion, sprouts, herbs and remaining dressing; toss gently to combine. Serve larb in lettuce leaves.
dressing place ingredients in screw-top jar; shake well.

preparation time 20 minutes **cooking time** 15 minutes **serves** 4
nutritional count per serving 26.9g total fat (8.3g saturated fat);
1852kJ (443 cal); 6.1g carbohydrate; 42.1g protein; 3.7g fibre

Thai lamb, eggplant and coriander stir-fry

1 tablespoon peanut oil
750g lamb strips
6 baby eggplants (360g), chopped coarsely
2 fresh small red thai chillies, chopped finely
1 medium brown onion (150g), chopped coarsely
2 cloves garlic, crushed
2 tablespoons grated palm sugar
2 tablespoons lime juice
1 tablespoon fish sauce
1 tablespoon light soy sauce
1 cup loosely packed fresh coriander leaves

1 Heat half the oil in wok; stir-fry lamb, in batches, until browned.
2 Heat remaining oil in wok; stir-fry eggplant until almost tender. Add chilli, onion and garlic; stir-fry until onion softens.
3 Return lamb to wok with sugar, juice and sauces; stir-fry until hot. Remove from heat; stir two-thirds of the coriander into stir-fry, sprinkle with remaining coriander.

preparation time 10 minutes **cooking time** 20 minutes **serves** 4
nutritional count per serving 21.4g total fat (8.3g saturated fat);
1722kJ (412 cal); 11.7g carbohydrate; 41.9g protein; 3.2g fibre

Cantonese lamb and pea stir-fry

1 tablespoon peanut oil
800g lamb strips
1 medium brown onion (150g), sliced thinly
1 clove garlic, crushed
150g snow peas, trimmed
150g sugar snap peas, trimmed
⅔ cup (80g) frozen peas
115g baby corn, halved lengthways
1 tablespoon dark soy sauce
1 tablespoon char siu sauce
¼ cup (60ml) chicken stock
1 tablespoon cornflour
2 tablespoons lime juice

1 Heat half the oil in wok; stir-fry lamb, in batches, until browned.
2 Heat remaining oil in wok; stir-fry onion and garlic until onion softens. Add peas and corn; stir-fry until corn is almost tender.
3 Return lamb to wok with sauces and stock; stir-fry about 2 minutes or until lamb is cooked. Stir in blended cornflour and juice; stir-fry until sauce boils and thickens.

preparation time 20 minutes **cooking time** 15 minutes **serves** 4
nutritional count per serving 23.2g total fat (8.9g saturated fat); 1977kJ (473 cal); 16g carbohydrate; 47.6g protein; 5.4g fibre
tip you can use lamb backstrap for this recipe, if you prefer; slice it thinly before use.

Crisp twice-fried lamb with thai basil

⅓ cup (80ml) sweet chilli sauce
¼ cup (60ml) oyster sauce
2 tablespoons light soy sauce
800g lamb strips
¾ cup (110g) plain flour
vegetable oil, for deep-frying
1 tablespoon vegetable oil, extra
1 small brown onion (80g), sliced thinly
2 cloves garlic, sliced thinly
250g sugar snap peas, trimmed
2 cups (160g) bean sprouts
1 cup loosely packed thai basil leaves

1 Combine sauces in small jug; pour two-thirds of the sauce mixture into medium bowl with lamb, mix well. Drain lamb; discard liquid.
2 Coat lamb in flour; shake off excess. Heat oil in wok; deep-fry lamb, in batches, until browned. Drain.
3 Heat extra oil in cleaned wok; stir-fry onion and garlic until onion softens. Add peas and remaining sauce mixture; stir-fry until peas are almost tender.
4 Return lamb to wok; stir-fry until hot. Remove from heat; stir in sprouts and basil.

preparation time 15 minutes **cooking time** 20 minutes **serves** 4
nutritional count per saving 34.5g total fat (10.2g saturated fat); 2713kJ (649 cal); 32.4g carbohydrate; 49.6g protein; 5.4g fibre

Chiang mai pork and eggplant

3 fresh small red thai chillies, halved
6 cloves garlic, quartered
1 medium brown onion (150g), chopped coarsely
500g baby eggplants
¼ cup (60ml) peanut oil
700g pork leg steaks, sliced thinly
1 tablespoon fish sauce
1 tablespoon dark soy sauce
1 tablespoon grated palm sugar
4 purple shallots (100g), sliced thinly
150g snake beans, cut into 5cm lengths
1 cup loosely packed thai basil leaves

1 Blend or process chilli, garlic and onion until mixture forms a paste.
2 Quarter eggplants lengthways; slice each piece into 5cm lengths. Cook eggplant in large saucepan of boiling water until just tender; drain, pat dry.
3 Heat half the oil in wok; stir-fry eggplant, in batches, until browned lightly. Drain.
4 Heat remaining oil in wok; stir-fry pork, in batches, until cooked.
5 Stir-fry garlic paste in wok about 3 minutes or until fragrant and browned lightly. Add sauces and sugar; stir-fry until sugar dissolves.
6 Add shallot and beans; stir-fry until beans are tender. Return eggplant and pork to wok; stir-fry until hot. Remove from heat; sprinkle with basil.

preparation time 20 minutes **cooking time** 25 minutes **serves** 4
nutritional count per serving 19.3g total fat (4.1g saturated fat);
1672kJ (400 cal); 10.1g carbohydrate; 43.6g protein; 5.8g fibre

Pork larb with broccolini

1 tablespoon peanut oil
2 cloves garlic, crushed
600g pork mince
⅓ cup (90g) grated palm sugar
2 tablespoons fish sauce
4 kaffir lime leaves, sliced finely
½ cup (40g) fried shallots
⅓ cup (45g) roasted unsalted peanuts
350g broccolini, trimmed, halved lengthways
1 tablespoon lime juice
1 cup loosely packed fresh coriander leaves
1 fresh long red chilli, sliced thinly
2 tablespoons coarsely chopped roasted unsalted peanuts

1 Heat oil in wok; stir-fry garlic and pork until pork is browned through. Remove from wok with slotted spoon.
2 Add sugar, sauce, lime leaves, shallots and nuts to wok; bring to the boil. Reduce heat; simmer, uncovered, 1 minute. Return pork to wok; cook, uncovered, about 2 minutes or until larb mixture is slightly dry and sticky.
3 Meanwhile, boil, steam or microwave broccolini; drain.
4 Stir juice and three-quarters of the coriander into larb off the heat; serve tossed with broccolini and sprinkled with remaining coriander, chilli and coarsely chopped nuts.

preparation time 15 minutes **cooking time** 10 minutes **serves** 4
nutritional count per serving 23.9g total fat (6g saturated fat); 2006kJ (480 cal); 25g carbohydrate; 39.5g protein; 5.5g fibre

Chilli orange pork stir-fry

2 tablespoons peanut oil
1kg pork fillets, sliced thinly
1 medium brown onion (150g), chopped coarsely
2 cloves garlic, crushed
1 fresh long red chilli, chopped finely
250g sugar snap peas, trimmed
¼ cup (60ml) light soy sauce
⅓ cup (80ml) sweet sherry
2 teaspoons finely grated orange rind
2 tablespoons orange juice
1 teaspoon cornflour

1 Heat half the oil in wok; stir-fry pork, in batches, until browned.
2 Heat remaining oil in wok; stir-fry onion, garlic and chilli until onion softens. Add peas; stir-fry until peas are just tender.
3 Return pork to wok with sauce, sherry, rind and blended juice and cornflour; stir-fry until sauce thickens slightly.

preparation time 15 minutes **cooking time** 15 minutes **serves** 6
nutritional count per serving 10g total fat (2.4g saturated fat); 1195kJ (286 cal); 5.9g carbohydrate; 38.8g protein; 1.5g fibre

Chilli pork with oyster sauce

1 tablespoon peanut oil
500g pork fillets, sliced thinly
1 clove garlic, crushed
1 medium white onion (150g), sliced thinly
1 large red capsicum (350g), sliced thinly
1 small green zucchini (90g), sliced thinly
1 small yellow zucchini (90g), sliced thinly
¼ cup (60ml) oyster sauce
1 tablespoon mild sweet chilli sauce
1 tablespoon coarsely chopped fresh coriander leaves

1 Heat oil in wok; stir-fry pork, in batches, until browned all over.
2 Stir-fry garlic and onion until onion is just tender. Add capsicum and zucchini; stir-fry until tender.
3 Return pork to wok with combined sauces; stir-fry until hot. Serve sprinkled with coriander.

preparation time 15 minutes **cooking time** 15 minutes **serves** 4
nutritional count per serving 8.1g total fat (1.9g saturated fat);
1012kJ (242 cal); 10.6g carbohydrate; 30.3g protein; 2.4g fibre

Stir-fried pork, buk choy and water chestnuts

¼ cup (60ml) light soy sauce
2 tablespoons oyster sauce
1 tablespoon honey
1 tablespoon chinese cooking wine
1 teaspoon five-spice powder
½ teaspoon sesame oil
1 clove garlic, crushed
600g pork fillets, sliced thinly
2 tablespoons peanut oil
600g baby buk choy, chopped coarsely
227g can water chestnuts, rinsed, drained, sliced thickly
½ cup (75g) unsalted roasted cashews
2 long green chillies, sliced thinly
1 tablespoon water

1 Combine 2 tablespoons of the soy sauce, 1 tablespoon of the oyster sauce, honey, wine, five-spice, sesame oil, garlic and pork in large bowl. Cover; refrigerate 3 hours or overnight.
2 Stir-fry pork mixture in oiled wok, in batches, until browned.
3 Heat peanut oil in same wok; stir-fry buk choy, water chestnuts, nuts and chilli until tender.
4 Return pork to wok with remaining soy and oyster sauces and the water; stir-fry until hot.

preparation time 15 minutes (plus refrigeration time)
cooking time 15 minutes **serves** 4
nutritional count per serving 23g total fat (4.5g saturated fat); 1827kJ (437 cal); 15.8g carbohydrate; 39.1g protein; 4.1g fibre

Sticky pork with vegies

1 tablespoon honey
2 tablespoons light soy sauce
2 tablespoons brown sugar
1 teaspoon five-spice powder
1 teaspoon hot chilli powder
3 cloves garlic, crushed
1 teaspoon sesame oil
750g pork neck, cut into 3cm cubes
2 tablespoons peanut oil
½ cup (70g) raw peanuts, chopped coarsely
1 medium carrot (120g), cut into matchsticks
150g snow peas, trimmed, sliced thinly lengthways
2 tablespoons orange juice
3 kaffir lime leaves, shredded
4 green onions, sliced thinly

1 Combine honey, sauce, sugar, five-spice, chilli, garlic and sesame oil in large bowl with pork. Cover; refrigerate 3 hours or overnight.
2 Heat half the peanut oil in wok; stir-fry nuts until browned. Drain.
3 Heat remaining oil in wok. Add pork; stir-fry, in batches, until browned. Return pork to wok with carrot; stir-fry until pork is cooked.
4 Add snow peas, juice and lime leaves; stir-fry until snow peas are tender. Remove from heat; toss in onion and nuts.

preparation time 15 minutes (plus refrigeration time)
cooking time 25 minutes **serves** 4
nutritional count per serving 33.7g total fat (8.1g saturated fat); 2366kJ (566 cal); 18.5g carbohydrate; 46.4g protein; 3.8g fibre

Sang choy bow

2 teaspoons sesame oil
1 small brown onion (80g), chopped finely
2 cloves garlic, crushed
2cm piece fresh ginger (10g), grated
500g lean pork mince
2 tablespoons water
100g shiitake mushrooms, chopped finely
2 tablespoons light soy sauce
2 tablespoons oyster sauce
1 tablespoon lime juice
2 cups bean sprouts
4 green onions, sliced thinly
¼ cup coarsely chopped fresh coriander
12 large butter lettuce leaves

1 Heat oil in wok; stir-fry brown onion, garlic and ginger until onion softens. Add pork; stir-fry until changed in colour.
2 Add the water, mushrooms, sauces and juice; stir-fry until mushrooms are tender. Remove from heat. Add sprouts, green onion and coriander; toss to combine.
3 Spoon sang choy bow into lettuce leaves to serve.

preparation time 15 minutes **cooking time** 15 minutes **serves** 4
nutritional count per serving 11.5g total fat (3.6g saturated fat); 1112kJ (266 cal); 8.9g carbohydrate; 29.3g protein; 4.1g fibre
tip the size of the butter lettuce available will determine whether you buy one or two of them in order to get a dozen large leaves. You could also use large iceberg leaves.

Pork with sweet and sour peaches

2 tablespoons cornflour
800g pork fillets, sliced thinly
2 tablespoons peanut oil
1 medium red onion (170g), chopped coarsely
1 medium red capsicum (200g), cut into thin strips
1 medium yellow capsicum (200g), cut into thin strips
⅓ cup (80ml) water
2 cloves garlic, crushed
2 tablespoons white sugar
2 tablespoons white wine vinegar
2 tablespoons tomato sauce
2 tablespoons light soy sauce
2 large peaches (440g), cut into wedges
⅓ cup coarsely chopped fresh coriander

1 Rub cornflour into pork in medium bowl.
2 Heat half the oil in wok; stir-fry pork, in batches, until browned.
3 Heat remaining oil in same wok; stir-fry onion and capsicums
until tender.
4 Return pork to wok with the water, garlic, sugar, vinegar and sauces;
stir-fry until pork is cooked. Add peach; stir-fry until hot. Remove from
heat; stir in coriander.

preparation time 20 minutes **cooking time** 10 minutes **serves** 4
nutritional count per serving 25.4g total fat (7.1g saturated fat);
2203kJ (527 cal); 26.9g carbohydrate; 45.9g protein; 3g fibre

Pork and lemon grass stir-fry

1 tablespoon peanut oil
2 tablespoons finely chopped lemon grass
2 fresh small red thai chillies, chopped finely
2cm piece fresh galangal (35g), chopped finely
2 cloves garlic, crushed
500g pork mince
1 tablespoon thai-style red curry paste
100g green beans, chopped coarsely
1 ½ tablespoons fish sauce
2 tablespoons lime juice
1 tablespoon grated palm sugar
1 small red onion (100g), sliced thinly
2 green onions, sliced thinly
¼ cup firmly packed fresh thai basil leaves
½ cup firmly packed fresh coriander leaves
¼ cup (75g) roasted peanuts, chopped coarsely
4 iceberg lettuce leaves

1 Heat oil in wok; cook lemon grass, chilli, galangal and garlic, stirring, until fragrant. Add pork; cook, stirring, until cooked through. Add curry paste; cook, stirring, until fragrant.
2 Add beans, fish sauce, juice and sugar to wok; cook, stirring, about 5 minutes or until beans are just tender. Remove from heat.
3 Add onions, basil, coriander and half the peanuts to pork mixture; stir to combine.
4 Serve pork mixture in lettuce cups sprinkled with remaining peanuts.

preparation time 15 minutes **cooking time** 20 minutes **serves** 4
nutritional count per serving 24.2g total fat (5.6g saturated fat);
1647kJ (394 cal); 9.5g carbohydrate; 32.4g protein; 5g fibre

Japanese pork stir-fry

2 tablespoons peanut oil
600g pork fillets, sliced thinly
1 large brown onion (200g), sliced thinly
1 medium red capsicum (200g), sliced thinly
1 medium green capsicum (200g), sliced thinly
200g green beans, chopped coarsely
2 cups (140g) coarsely shredded wombok
¼ cup (60ml) tonkatsu sauce
¼ cup (60ml) sukiyaki sauce

1 Heat half the oil in wok; stir-fry pork, in batches, until browned all over.
2 Heat remaining oil in same wok; stir-fry onion until just tender. Add capsicums and beans; stir-fry until just tender.
3 Return pork to wok with wombok and sauces; stir-fry until wombok is just wilted.

preparation time 15 minutes **cooking time** 10 minutes **serves** 4
nutritional count per serving 13.7g total fat (3g saturated fat);
1425kJ (341 cal); 13g carbohydrate; 36.6g protein; 5g fibre

Chilli fried rice with chicken and broccolini

You need to cook 1 cup (200g) white long-grain rice for this recipe. You need a large barbecued chicken, weighing about 900g for this recipe.

1 tablespoon peanut oil
3 eggs, beaten lightly
1 medium brown onion (150g), sliced thinly
1 clove garlic, crushed
2 fresh long red chillies, sliced thinly
175g broccolini, chopped coarsely
2 cups (320g) shredded barbecued chicken
3 cups cooked white long-grain rice
1 tablespoon light soy sauce
1 tablespoon hoisin sauce

1 Heat about a third of the oil in wok; add half the egg, cook over medium heat, tilting pan, until almost set. Remove omelette from wok; roll tightly, slice thinly. Repeat process using another third of the oil and remaining egg.
2 Heat remaining oil in wok; stir-fry onion, garlic and chilli until onion softens. Add broccolini; stir-fry until tender.
3 Add remaining ingredients to wok; stir-fry until hot. Add omelette; toss gently to combine.

preparation time 10 minutes **cooking time** 15 minutes **serves** 4
nutritional count per serving 15.3g total fat (3.8g saturated fat); 1881kJ (450 cal); 44.6g carbohydrate; 30.9g protein; 4.1g fibre

Hokkien mee

450g hokkien noodles
1 tablespoon peanut oil
600g piece beef eye fillet, sliced thinly
1 medium brown onion (150g), sliced thinly
2 cloves garlic, crushed
1 medium red capsicum (200g), sliced thinly
115g baby corn, halved lengthways
150g snow peas, trimmed, halved diagonally
2 baby buk choy (300g), chopped coarsely
¼ cup (60ml) char siu sauce
1 tablespoon dark soy sauce
¼ cup (60ml) chicken stock

1 Place noodles in medium heatproof bowl, cover with boiling water; separate with fork, drain.
2 Heat half the oil in wok; stir-fry beef, in batches, until browned.
3 Heat remaining oil in wok; stir-fry onion, garlic and capsicum until tender.
4 Return beef to wok with noodles, corn, snow peas, buk choy, sauces and stock; stir-fry until vegetables are tender and beef is cooked.

preparation time 15 minutes **cooking time** 15 minutes **serves** 4
nutritional count per serving 10.8g total fat (4.6g saturated fat); 1129kJ (270 cal); 25.2g carbohydrate; 25.7g protein; 4.4g fibre

Sweet soy fried noodles

450g fresh wide rice noodles
1 tablespoon peanut oil
3 cloves garlic, sliced thinly
2 eggs, beaten lightly
280g gai lan, chopped coarsely
200g snake beans, cut into 5cm lengths
⅓ cup (80ml) kecap manis
2 tablespoons light soy sauce
½ teaspoon dried chilli flakes
350g packet fried tofu, cut into 2cm cubes
4 green onions, sliced thinly
¾ cup loosely packed thai basil leaves

1 Place noodles in large heatproof bowl, cover with boiling water;
separate with fork, drain.
2 Heat oil in wok; stir-fry garlic until fragrant. Add egg; stir-fry until set.
Add vegetables, sauces and chilli; stir-fry until vegetables are tender.
3 Add noodles, tofu, onion and basil; stir-fry until hot.

preparation time 15 minutes **cooking time** 20 minutes **serves** 4
nutritional count per serving 18.2g total fat (4g saturated fat);
2036kJ (487 cal); 55.4g carbohydrate; 20.1g protein; 9.8g fibre
tips known as "pad sieu" this traditional Thai dish is similar to the
famous "pad thai", but uses kecap manis, a thick, sweet soy sauce,
to give it its special flavour.
We used a packaged fried tofu, which can be bought from Asian food
shops and some supermarkets. To make it yourself, simply shallow-fry
cubes of drained firm silken tofu in vegetable oil until just browned; drain
well before tossing with vegetables.

Chicken fried rice

You need to cook 2 cups (400g) white long-grain rice the day before making this recipe; spread rice evenly onto a tray, refrigerate overnight.

1 tablespoon vegetable oil
2 eggs, beaten lightly
3 rashers rindless bacon (195g), chopped coarsely
2 cloves garlic, crushed
2cm piece fresh ginger (10g), grated
1½ cups (240g) coarsely chopped leftover cooked chicken
4 cups cold cooked rice
1 cup (140g) frozen pea and corn mixture
¼ cup (60ml) light soy sauce
1 cup (80g) bean sprouts
6 green onions, sliced thinly

1 Heat half the oil in wok. Pour egg into wok; cook over medium heat, tilting pan, until almost set. Remove omelette from wok; roll tightly, slice thinly.
2 Heat remaining oil in wok; stir-fry bacon, garlic and ginger until bacon is crisp.
3 Add chicken to wok; stir-fry 1 minute. Add rice, frozen vegetables and sauce; stir-fry until hot. Add sprouts, onion and omelette; stir-fry 1 minute.

preparation time 10 minutes **cooking time** 15 minutes **serves** 4
nutritional count per serving 21.9g total fat (5.9g saturated fat); 2362kJ (565 cal); 52.6g carbohydrate; 37.2g protein; 3.8g fibre
tip packages of mixed frozen peas and corn are found in most supermarkets.

Balinese chilli lamb and fried noodles

600g hokkien noodles
1 tablespoon sambal oelek
1 tablespoon dark soy sauce
1 tablespoon fish sauce
2 cloves garlic, crushed
750g lamb backstraps, sliced thinly
¼ cup (60ml) peanut oil
⅓ cup (55g) coarsely chopped brazil nuts
⅔ cup (160ml) beef stock
2 tablespoons oyster sauce
2 tablespoons lime juice
2 teaspoons brown sugar
150g sugar snap peas, trimmed
⅓ cup finely chopped fresh mint
2 fresh small red thai chillies, chopped finely

1 Place noodles in large heatproof bowl, cover with boiling water; separate with fork, drain.
2 Combine sambal, sauces and garlic in large bowl with lamb.
3 Heat half a teaspoon of oil in wok; stir-fry nuts until browned lightly. Remove from wok.
4 Heat 2 tablespoons of remaining oil in wok; stir-fry lamb, in batches, until browned.
5 Heat remaining oil in wok; stir-fry noodles until browned lightly.
6 Add stock, oyster sauce, juice and sugar to wok; simmer about 3 minutes or until sauce thickens slightly.
7 Return lamb to wok with peas; stir-fry until hot. Serve noodles topped with lamb mixture and sprinkled with nuts, mint and chilli.

preparation time 15 minutes **cooking time** 10 minutes **serves** 4
nutritional count per serving 40.5g total fat (12.1g saturated fat); 3164kJ (757 cal); 45.4g carbohydrate; 50.2g protein; 5.4g fibre

Javanese stir-fried pork and rice noodles

450g fresh wide rice noodles
1 tablespoon vegetable oil
500g pork mince
2 cloves garlic, crushed
1 tablespoon sambal oelek
4 green onions, sliced thinly
⅓ cup (80ml) kecap manis
2 baby buk choy (300g), leaves separated
1 cup loosely packed fresh coriander leaves

1 Place noodles in large heatproof bowl, cover with boiling water;
separate with fork, drain.
2 Heat oil in wok; stir-fry pork until browned. Add garlic, sambal, onion
and 1 tablespoon of the kecap manis; stir-fry 1 minute.
3 Add noodles, remaining kecap manis and buk choy to wok; stir-fry
until hot. Sprinkle with coriander.

preparation time 10 minutes **cooking time** 15 minutes **serves** 4
nutritional count per serving 14.5g total fat (3.8g saturated fat);
1927kJ (461 cal); 49g carbohydrate; 31.1g protein; 2.8g fibre

Barbecued pork with hokkien noodles

1 tablespoon peanut oil
4 green onions, chopped coarsely
2 cloves garlic, sliced thinly
1 medium red capsicum (200g), sliced thinly
½ cup (190g) char siu sauce
2 tablespoons sambal oelek
¼ cup (60ml) water
2 tablespoons lime juice
4cm piece fresh ginger (20g), grated
1 cup (120g) frozen peas
400g chinese barbecued pork, sliced thinly
440g fresh thin hokkien noodles

1 Heat oil in wok; stir-fry onion, garlic and capsicum 1 minute.
2 Add remaining ingredients; stir-fry until peas are just cooked and mixture is hot.

preparation time 10 minutes **cooking time** 10 minutes **serves** 4
nutritional count per serving 7.4g total fat (1.2g saturated fat);
719kJ (172 cal); 22.3g carbohydrate; 1.9g protein; 5.9g fibre

Curried fried rice with pork and prawns

You need to cook about ⅔ cup (130g) white long-grain rice for this recipe.

800g pork leg steaks, sliced thinly
1 tablespoon white sugar
2 tablespoons light soy sauce
125g uncooked small prawns
2 tablespoons peanut oil
2 eggs, beaten lightly
1 teaspoon curry powder
2 cloves garlic, crushed
2 cups cold cooked white long-grain rice
4 green onions, sliced thinly
2 cups (240g) frozen pea and corn mixture

1 Combine pork in medium bowl with sugar and half the sauce. Shell and devein prawns, leaving tails intact.
2 Heat 1 teaspoon of the oil in wok. Pour egg into wok; cook over medium heat, tilting pan, until almost set. Remove omelette from wok; roll tightly, slice thinly.
3 Heat 2 teaspoons of the remaining oil in wok; stir-fry pork, in batches, until cooked as desired.
4 Heat 1 teaspoon of remaining oil in wok; stir-fry prawns until just changed in colour. Remove from wok.
5 Heat remaining oil in wok; cook curry powder and garlic, stirring, until fragrant. Add rice, onion, frozen vegetables and remaining sauce; stir-fry until vegetables are just tender.
6 Return pork, prawns and half the omelette to wok; stir-fry until heated through. Sprinkle fried rice with remaining omelette.

preparation time 20 minutes   **cooking time** 25 minutes   **serves** 4
nutritional count per serving 18.1g total fat (4.3g saturated fat); 2337kJ (559 cal); 38g carbohydrate; 57.5g protein; 4.9g fibre
tip packages of mixed frozen peas and corn are found in most supermarkets.

Chicken mee goreng

450g wide fresh rice noodles
1 tablespoon peanut oil
600g chicken thigh fillets, sliced thinly
2 cloves garlic, crushed
1 medium red capsicum (200g), sliced thinly
500g baby buk choy, leaves separated
⅓ cup (80ml) oyster sauce
1 tablespoon light soy sauce
½ cup (75g) roasted unsalted cashews, chopped coarsely
¼ cup loosely packed fresh coriander leaves

1 Place noodles in large heatproof bowl; cover with boiling water, separate with fork, drain.
2 Heat half the oil in wok; cook chicken, in batches, until browned.
3 Heat remaining oil in wok; stir-fry garlic until fragrant. Add capsicum, buk choy and sauces; stir-fry until vegetables are tender.
4 Return chicken to wok with noodles; stir-fry until chicken is cooked. Remove from heat; sprinkle with nuts and coriander.

preparation time 10 minutes **cooking time** 15 minutes **serves** 4
nutritional count per serving 25.6g total fat (5.8g saturated fat);
2211kJ (529 cal); 35.8g carbohydrate; 36.6g protein; 4.2g fibre

Nasi goreng

You need to cook 2 cups (400g) white long-grain rice the day before making this recipe; spread rice evenly onto a tray, refrigerate overnight.

720g cooked medium king prawns
1 tablespoon peanut oil
175g dried chinese sausages, sliced thickly
1 medium brown onion (150g), sliced thinly
1 medium red capsicum (200g), sliced thinly
2 fresh long red chillies, sliced thinly
2 cloves garlic, crushed
2cm piece fresh ginger (10g), grated
1 teaspoon shrimp paste
4 cups (600g) cold cooked white long-grain rice
2 tablespoons kecap manis
1 tablespoon light soy sauce
4 green onions, sliced thinly
1 tablespoon peanut oil, extra
4 eggs

1 Shell and devein prawns.
2 Heat half the oil in wok; stir-fry sausage, in batches, until browned.
3 Heat remaining oil in wok; stir-fry onion, capsicum, chilli, garlic, ginger and paste, until vegetables soften. Add prawns and rice; stir-fry 2 minutes.
4 Return sausage to wok with sauces and half the green onion; stir-fry until combined.
5 Heat extra oil in large frying pan; fry eggs, one side only, until just set.
6 Divide nasi goreng among serving bowls, top each with an egg; sprinkle with remaining green onion.

preparation time 25 minutes **cooking time** 15 minutes **serves** 4
nutritional count per serving 25.7g total fat (7.4g saturated fat); 2730kJ (653 cal); 48.5g carbohydrate; 54.7g protein; 3.3g fibre
tip dried chinese sausage, also called lop chong, is usually made from pork and sold, strung together, in Asian food shops.

Singapore curry noodles

You need to purchase a large barbecued chicken weighing about 900g for this recipe.

1 small brown onion (80g), sliced thinly
2 rashers rindless bacon (130g), chopped finely
2 teaspoons curry powder
3 cups (480g) shredded barbecued chicken
6 green onions, sliced thinly
2 tablespoons soy sauce
⅓ cup (80ml) sweet sherry
3cm piece fresh ginger (15g), grated
400g fresh thin rice noodles

1 Heat wok; stir-fry brown onion and bacon until bacon is crisp. Add curry powder; stir-fry until fragrant.
2 Add chicken, green onion, sauce, sherry and ginger; stir-fry to combine. Add noodles; stir-fry, tossing gently, until hot.

preparation time 10 minutes **cooking time** 10 minutes **serves** 4
nutritional count per serving 12.9g total fat (4.1g saturated fat); 1517kJ (363 cal); 25.9g carbohydrate; 30.1g protein; 1.4g fibre

Ginger-plum chicken and noodle stir-fry

2 tablespoons vegetable oil
600g chicken breast fillets, sliced thinly
450g hokkien noodles
1 medium brown onion (150g), sliced thinly
1 clove garlic, crushed
3cm piece fresh ginger (15g), grated
400g packaged fresh asian stir-fry vegetables
2 tablespoons sweet chilli sauce
2 tablespoons plum sauce

1 Heat half the oil in wok; stir-fry chicken, in batches, until browned.
2 Meanwhile, place noodles in medium heatproof bowl, cover with boiling water; separate with fork, drain.
3 Heat remaining oil in wok; stir-fry onion, garlic and ginger until onion softens. Add vegetables; stir-fry until just tender.
4 Return chicken to wok with noodles and sauces; stir-fry until hot.

preparation time 10 minutes **cooking time** 15 minutes **serves** 4
nutritional count per serving 19.4g total fat (4.6g saturated fat);
2784kJ (666 cal); 73.3g carbohydrate; 45.6g protein; 6.2g fibre

Chorizo fried rice

You need to cook about 1½ cups (300g) of white long-grain rice the day before making this recipe. Spread it in an even layer on a tray and refrigerate overnight. You will also need a quarter of a small wombok.

1 teaspoon vegetable oil
2 eggs, beaten lightly
2 chorizo sausages (340g), sliced thinly
1 fresh long red chilli, sliced thinly
1 clove garlic, crushed
2cm piece fresh ginger (10g), grated
2 cups (160g) coarsely shredded wombok
1 cup (120g) frozen pea, corn and carrot mixture
3 cups cold cooked rice
2 tablespoons dark soy sauce

1 Heat oil in wok. Pour egg into wok; cook over medium heat, tilting pan, until almost set. Remove omelette from wok; roll tightly, slice thinly.
2 Add chorizo to wok; stir-fry about 5 minutes or until crisp. Add chilli, garlic, ginger, wombok and frozen vegetables; stir-fry about 5 minutes or until vegetables just soften.
3 Add rice, omelette and sauce to wok; stir-fry until combined and heated through.

preparation time 15 minutes **cooking time** 20 minutes **serves** 4
nutritional count per serving 28.5g total fat (9.8g saturated fat); 2278kJ (545 cal); 47.2g carbohydrate; 23.4g protein; 3.6g fibre

Pad thai

540g uncooked medium king prawns
¼ cup (85g) tamarind concentrate
⅓ cup (80ml) sweet chilli sauce
2 tablespoons fish sauce
⅓ cup firmly packed fresh coriander leaves
¼ cup (35g) roasted unsalted peanuts
¼ cup (20g) fried shallots
2 cups (160g) bean sprouts
4 green onions, sliced thinly
375g dried rice stick noodles
1 tablespoon peanut oil
2 cloves garlic, crushed
4cm piece fresh ginger (20g), grated
3 fresh small red thai chillies, chopped finely
250g pork mince
2 eggs, beaten lightly
1 lime, quartered

1 Shell and devein prawns, leaving tails intact.
2 Combine tamarind and sauces in small jug.
3 Combine coriander, nuts, shallots, half the sprouts and half the onion in medium bowl.
4 Place noodles in large heatproof bowl, cover with boiling water; stand until just tender, drain.
5 Meanwhile, heat oil in wok; stir-fry garlic, ginger and chilli until fragrant. Add pork; stir-fry until cooked. Add prawns; stir-fry 1 minute. Add egg; stir-fry until set. Add tamarind mixture, remaining sprouts and onion, and noodles; stir-fry until combined.
6 Divide mixture among serving bowls; sprinkle with coriander mixture, serve with lime wedges.

preparation time 25 minutes **cooking time** 10 minutes **serves** 4
nutritional count per serving 17.5g total fat (3.9g saturated fat);
1827kJ (437 cal); 30.3g carbohydrate; 36.8g protein; 4.9g fibre

Hokkien noodle stir-fry

600g hokkien noodles
600g lamb strips
2 tablespoons cornflour
1 teaspoon salt
¼ cup (60ml) peanut oil
1 medium brown onion (150g), sliced thickly
1 clove garlic, crushed
1cm piece fresh ginger (5g), grated
1 large red capsicum (350g), sliced thinly
200g snow peas, trimmed, halved
⅓ cup (80ml) plum sauce
¼ cup (60ml) oyster sauce
¼ cup (60ml) chicken stock
2 teaspoons tamarind concentrate

1 Place noodles in large heatproof bowl; cover with boiling water, separate with fork, drain.
2 Combine lamb, cornflour and salt in large bowl.
3 Heat 1 tablespoon of the oil in wok; stir-fry lamb mixture, in batches, until browned all over.
4 Heat remaining oil in same wok; stir-fry onion, garlic and ginger until onion softens. Add capsicum and snow peas; stir-fry until just tender.
5 Return lamb to wok with noodles, sauces, stock and paste; stir-fry until heated through.

preparation time 15 minutes **cooking time** 15 minutes **serves** 4
nutritional count per serving 28g total fat (8.5g saturated fat); 2817kJ (674 cal); 64.4g carbohydrate; 41.2g protein; 5.4g fibre

Noodles and buk choy with mixed garlic mushrooms

600g fresh thin egg noodles
2 tablespoons peanut oil
1 tablespoon finely grated lemon rind
1 teaspoon dried chilli flakes
2 baby buk choy, leaves separated
¼ cup (60ml) lemon juice
4 cloves garlic, crushed
150g oyster mushrooms, halved
100g fresh shiitake mushrooms, halved
200g swiss brown mushrooms, halved
2 tablespoons kecap manis

1 Place noodles in large heatproof bowl, cover with boiling water; separate noodles with fork, drain.
2 Heat half the oil in wok; stir-fry rind and chilli until fragrant. Add noodles, buk choy and juice; stir-fry until buk choy is wilted. Remove from wok; cover to keep warm.
3 Heat remaining oil in wok; cook garlic, stirring, until fragrant. Add mushrooms and kecap manis; stir-fry until mushrooms soften.
4 Serve mushrooms on noodles.

preparation time 10 minutes **cooking time** 20 minutes **serves** 4
nutritional count per serving 11.5g total fat (2g saturated fat); 1033kJ (247 cal); 84.5g carbohydrate; 20.3g protein; 9.2g fibre

Stir-fry beef and noodles

750g piece beef rump, sliced thinly
¼ cup (60ml) fish sauce
⅓ cup (80ml) oyster sauce
⅓ cup (80ml) sweet chilli sauce
3 cloves garlic, crushed
500g hokkien noodles
2 tablespoons peanut oil
2 large brown onions (400g), sliced thinly
200g snow peas
1 cup (80g) bean sprouts
1 fresh long red chilli, sliced thinly

1 Combine beef with half the combined sauces and garlic in large bowl. Cover; refrigerate 3 hours or overnight.
2 Place noodles in large heatproof bowl, cover with boiling water; separate noodles with fork, drain.
3 Heat half the oil in wok; stir-fry beef mixture, in batches, until browned all over and almost cooked.
4 Heat remaining oil in wok; stir-fry onion until soft. Add snow peas and sprouts; stir-fry 1 minute. Return beef and noodles to wok with remaining combined sauces and garlic; stir-fry until hot. Serve sprinkled with chilli.

preparation time 10 minutes (plus refrigeration time)
cooking time 15 minutes **serves** 4
nutritional count per serving 21.6g total fat (6.5g saturated fat); 2541kJ (608 cal); 48.9g carbohydrate; 50.5g protein; 6.8g fibre

Sweet chilli plum chicken with noodles

¼ cup (60ml) sweet chilli sauce
2 tablespoons plum sauce
750g chicken thigh fillets, sliced thinly
450g hokkien noodles
227g can water chestnuts, rinsed, halved
8 green onions, sliced thickly
1 fresh long red chilli, sliced thinly
2 cloves garlic, crushed
300g buk choy, trimmed, chopped coarsely

1 Combine sauces in large bowl with chicken. Cover; refrigerate 1 hour.
2 Heat oiled wok; stir-fry chicken mixture, in batches, until browned.
3 Meanwhile, place noodles in medium heatproof bowl; cover with boiling water, separate with fork, drain.
4 Stir-fry chestnuts, onion, chilli and garlic in wok 2 minutes.
5 Return chicken to wok with buk choy; stir-fry until chicken is cooked. Serve with noodles.

preparation time 20 minutes (plus refrigeration time)
cooking time 20 minutes **serves** 4
nutritional count per serving 14.9g total fat (4.2g saturated fat); 2011kJ (481 cal); 43.1g carbohydrate; 41g protein; 5.4g fibre

Coconut rice with capsicum and coriander

½ cup (40g) shredded coconut
2 tablespoons vegetable oil
2 teaspoons chilli oil
1 medium brown onion (150g), chopped coarsely
1 medium red capsicum (200g), chopped coarsely
3 cloves garlic, crushed
3cm piece fresh ginger (15g), grated
1½ cups (300g) calrose rice
1½ cups (375ml) chicken stock
1 cup (250ml) water
140ml can coconut milk
3 green onions, chopped coarsely
¼ cup coarsely chopped fresh coriander
¼ cup (60ml) lemon juice
¼ cup fresh coriander leaves

1 Heat wok; add coconut, stir constantly until browned lightly. Remove from wok.
2 Heat oils in wok; stir-fry brown onion, capsicum, garlic and ginger until onion softens. Add rice; stir-fry 2 minutes.
3 Add stock, the water and coconut milk to wok; simmer, covered, about 20 minutes or until liquid is absorbed and rice is tender.
4 Remove from heat; stir in green onion, chopped coriander, juice and half the coconut. Sprinkle with remaining coconut and coriander leaves.

preparation time 15 minutes **cooking time** 20 minutes **serves** 4
nutritional count per serving 26.2g total fat (13.9g saturated fat);
2282kJ (546 cal); 66.4g carbohydrate; 9g protein; 4.5g fibre

Quick pork fried rice

You need to cook about 1 cup (200g) of white long-grain rice the day before making this recipe. Spread it in an even layer on a tray and refrigerate overnight.

1 tablespoon honey
2 tablespoons kecap manis
600g pork fillets, sliced thinly
2 teaspoons peanut oil
2 eggs, beaten lightly
1 medium carrot (120g), cut into matchstick-sized pieces
1 medium red capsicum (200g), sliced thinly
3 cups cooked white long-grain rice
8 green onions, sliced thinly
1 cup (80g) bean sprouts
2 tablespoons soy sauce
2 tablespoons char siu sauce

1 Combine honey and kecap manis in medium bowl with pork.
2 Heat half the oil in wok. Pour egg into wok; cook over medium heat, tilting pan, until almost set. Remove omelette from wok; roll tightly, slice thinly.
3 Heat remaining oil in wok; stir-fry pork, in batches, until cooked.
4 Stir-fry carrot and capsicum in wok until just tender.
5 Return half the omelette to wok with rice, pork, onion, sprouts and sauces; stir-fry until hot. Remove from heat; sprinkle with remaining omelette.

preparation time 20 minutes **cooking time** 15 minutes **serves** 4
nutritional count per serving 9.4g total fat (2.5g saturated fat);
2032kJ (486 cal); 54.6g carbohydrate; 42.6g protein; 4.7g fibre

Noodles with vegetables and cream

375g dried rice stick noodles
1 tablespoon olive oil
1 small brown onion (80g), cut into wedges
2 baby fennel bulbs (260g), trimmed, sliced thinly
1 clove garlic, crushed
200g mushrooms, sliced thickly
2 small zucchini (180g), sliced thinly
300ml cream
150g snow peas, trimmed, sliced thinly
150g sugar snap peas, trimmed, sliced thinly
½ cup shredded fresh basil
2 tablespoons finely chopped dill leaves
¼ cup loosely packed fresh basil leaves

1 Place noodles in large heatproof bowl, cover with boiling water; stand until tender, drain.
2 Meanwhile, heat oil in wok; stir-fry onion, fennel and garlic until vegetables are tender. Remove from wok.
3 Stir-fry mushrooms and zucchini in wok until browned lightly. Return fennel mixture to wok with cream; bring to the boil. Stir-fry until sauce thickens slightly. Add noodles and peas; stir-fry until hot. Remove from heat; stir in herbs.

preparation time 15 minutes **cooking time** 10 minutes **serves** 6
nutritional count per serving 25.3g total fat (14.7g saturated fat);
1396kJ (334 cal); 19.7g carbohydrate; 5.8g protein; 3.9g fibre

Fried noodles with sausage and cabbage

450g wide fresh rice noodles
2 teaspoons peanut oil
300g dried chinese sausages, sliced thickly
1 medium brown onion (150g), chopped coarsely
2 cloves garlic, crushed
100g shiitake mushrooms, chopped coarsely
1 small wombok (700g), chopped coarsely
¼ cup (60ml) chicken stock
¼ cup (95g) char siu sauce
2 tablespoons lime juice
½ cup loosely packed fresh coriander leaves
¼ cup loosely packed fresh mint leaves
⅓ cup (50g) coarsely chopped roasted unsalted cashews
1 fresh long red chilli, sliced thinly

1 Place noodles in large heatproof bowl, cover with boiling water; separate with fork, drain.
2 Heat oil in wok; stir-fry sausage, onion, garlic and mushrooms until sausage is browned and vegetables tender.
3 Add wombok; stir-fry until wombok is wilted. Add stock, sauce, juice and noodles; stir-fry until hot. Remove from heat; sprinkle with coriander and mint. Serve with nuts and chilli.

preparation time 25 minutes **cooking time** 10 minutes **serves** 4
nutritional count per serving 28.4g total fat (7.8g saturated fat); 2161kJ (517 cal); 43.6g carbohydrate; 17.6g protein; 9.8g fibre
tip dried chinese sausage, also called lop chong, is usually made from pork and sold, strung together, in Asian food shops.

Fried rice

You need to cook about 1 cup (200g) of white long-grain rice the day before making this recipe. Spread it in an even layer on a tray and refrigerate overnight.

1 tablespoon peanut oil
2 eggs, beaten lightly
120g baby corn, halved
1 trimmed celery stick (75g), chopped finely
1 small red capsicum (150g), chopped finely
2 cloves garlic, crushed
140g ham, chopped coarsely
3 cups cooked long-grain white rice
1 tablespoon kecap manis
4 green onions, sliced thinly

1 Heat half the oil in wok. Pour egg into wok; cook over medium heat, tilting pan, until almost set. Remove omelette from wok; roll tightly, slice thinly.
2 Heat remaining oil in wok; stir-fry corn and celery 2 minutes. Add capsicum, garlic and ham; stir-fry 2 minutes. Add rice and kecap manis; stir-fry until heated through. Stir in onion and omelette.

preparation time 10 minutes **cooking time** 10 minutes **serves** 4
nutritional count per serving 9.4g total fat (2.2g saturated fat); 1430kJ (342 cal); 47.1g carbohydrate; 15.2g protein; 3.2g fibre

Chilli beef and vegetables with noodles

4 cloves garlic, crushed
¼ cup (60ml) fish sauce
1 tablespoon soy sauce
2 tablespoons oyster sauce
3 fresh small red thai chillies, chopped finely
2 teaspoons brown sugar
10cm stick fresh lemon grass (20g), chopped finely
¼ cup coarsely chopped fresh coriander
500g piece beef fillet, sliced thinly
450g thick rice noodles
2 teaspoons peanut oil
6 spring onions (150g), trimmed, quartered
150g snow peas
340g baby buk choy
2 medium tomatoes (300g), cut into wedges

1 Combine garlic, sauces, chilli, sugar, lemon grass and coriander in
large bowl with beef. Cover, refrigerate 3 hours or overnight.
2 Place noodles in medium heatproof bowl, cover with boiling water;
stand until just tender, drain.
3 Heat oil in wok; stir-fry beef mixture, in batches, until browned all over.
Add onions to wok; stir-fry until onions are browned lightly.
4 Add snow peas, buk choy, tomatoes, noodles and beef mixture to wok;
cook, stirring, until heated through.
5 Serve sprinkled with extra fresh coriander leaves, if desired.

preparation time 20 minutes (plus refrigeration time)
cooking time 15 minutes **serves** 4
nutritional count per serving 10.9g total fat (3.6g saturated);
1626kJ (389 cal); 35.6g carbohydrate; 34.1g protein; 5.1g fibre
tip scotch fillet, eye-fillet or rump steak can be used for this recipe.

Sukiyaki

400g fresh udon noodles
300g fresh firm silken tofu
4 eggs
¼ cup (60ml) vegetable oil
600g beef rump steak, trimmed, sliced thinly
8 oyster mushrooms
4 green onions, sliced thinly
300g spinach, trimmed, chopped coarsely
2 cups (160g) bean sprouts
broth
1 cup (250ml) japanese soy sauce
½ cup (125ml) sake
½ cup (125ml) mirin
½ cup (125ml) water
½ cup (110g) white sugar
2 cloves garlic, crushed

1 Cook ingredients for broth in medium saucepan over medium heat, stirring, until sugar dissolves. Remove from heat; cover to keep warm.
2 Place noodles in heatproof bowl, cover with boiling water; separate with fork, drain. Cut into random lengths.
3 Cut tofu into 2cm cubes; spread, in single layer, on absorbent-paper-lined-tray. Cover tofu with more absorbent paper, stand 10 minutes.
4 Break eggs into individual serving bowls; beat lightly.
5 Heat half the oil in wok; stir-fry beef, in batches, until browned.
6 Heat half the remaining oil in wok; stir-fry tofu, in batches, until browned.
7 Add remaining oil to wok; stir-fry mushrooms, onion, spinach and sprouts until vegetables are just tender.
8 Return beef and tofu to wok with noodles and broth; stir-fry until hot. Serve sukiyaki from wok, with each diner using chopsticks to pick up sukiyaki ingredients and dip in their individual bowl of egg and eat.

preparation time 20 minutes **cooking time** 10 minutes **serves** 4
nutritional count per serving 52g total fat (17.2g saturated fat); 4811kJ (1151 cal); 87.4g carbohydrate; 65.7g protein; 13.6g fibre

Beef chow mein

1 tablespoon vegetable oil
500g beef mince
1 medium brown onion (150g), chopped finely
2 cloves garlic, crushed
1 tablespoon curry powder
1 large carrot (180g), chopped finely
2 trimmed celery stalks (200g), sliced thinly
150g mushrooms, sliced thinly
1 cup (250ml) chicken stock
⅓ cup (80ml) oyster sauce
2 tablespoons dark soy sauce
440g thin fresh egg noodles
½ cup (60g) frozen peas
½ small wombok (350g), shredded coarsely

1 Heat oil in wok; stir-fry beef, onion and garlic until beef is browned. Add curry powder; stir-fry about 1 minute or until fragrant. Add carrot, celery and mushrooms; stir-fry until vegetables soften.
2 Add stock, sauces and noodles; stir-fry 2 minutes. Add peas and wombok; stir-fry until wombok just wilts.

preparation time 30 minutes **cooking time** 20 minutes **serves** 4
nutritional count per serving 15.7g total fat (4.6g saturated fat); 2571kJ (615 cal); 70.6g carbohydrate; 42.3g protein; 8.4g fibre

Mixed mushrooms and chicken with crispy noodles

1 tablespoon peanut oil
1kg chicken thigh fillets, sliced thinly
2 cloves garlic, crushed
8 green onions, chopped coarsely
200g shiitake mushrooms, chopped coarsely
200g gai lan, chopped coarsely
100g oyster mushrooms, chopped coarsely
⅓ cup (80ml) vegetarian mushroom oyster sauce
100g enoki mushrooms
50g packet fried noodles

1 Heat oil in wok; stir-fry chicken, in batches, until cooked.
2 Return chicken to wok with garlic and onion; stir-fry until onion softens. Add shiitake mushrooms; stir-fry until tender. Add gai lan, oyster mushrooms and sauce; stir-fry until vegetables are tender.
3 Remove from heat; toss in enoki mushrooms and noodles.

preparation time 15 minutes **cooking time** 20 minutes **serves** 4
nutritional count per serving 24.3g total fat (7g saturated fat); 2065kJ (494 cal); 15.9g carbohydrate; 51.1g protein; 4.5g fibre

Thai lamb and noodle stir-fry

200g thick rice stick noodles
2 tablespoons peanut oil
500g lamb strips
1 tablespoon finely chopped lemon grass
1 fresh long red chilli, sliced thinly
2 cloves garlic, crushed
1 large brown onion (200g), sliced thinly
250g snake beans, cut into 5cm lengths
⅓ cup (80ml) sweet chilli sauce
2 tablespoons fish sauce
¼ cup (60ml) chicken stock
¼ cup firmly packed fresh mint leaves
¼ cup (35g) toasted salted peanuts

1 Place noodles in large heatproof bowl, cover with boiling water, stand until just tender; drain.
2 Meanwhile, heat half the oil in wok; stir-fry lamb, in batches, until browned all over.
3 Heat remaining oil in wok; stir-fry lemon grass, chilli, garlic and onion until tender. Add beans; stir-fry until almost tender.
4 Return lamb to wok with sauces, stock and noodles; stir fry until hot. Add mint, toss gently. Serve immediately, sprinkled with peanuts.

preparation time 15 minutes **cooking time** 15 minutes **serves** 4
nutritional count per serving 25.8g total fat (7.3g saturated fat);
2303kJ (531 cal); 41.5g carbohydrate; 35.4g protein; 5.4g fibre

Five-spice tofu with egg noodles and lemon chilli sauce

½ cup (125ml) sweet chilli sauce
2 teaspoons finely grated lemon rind
¼ cup (60ml) lemon juice
440g packet fresh egg noodles
⅓ cup (50g) plain flour
2 teaspoons five-spice powder
300g firm tofu, cut into 2cm pieces
1 tablespoon olive oil
1 large brown onion (200g), chopped coarsely
3 cloves garlic, sliced thinly
1 small yellow capsicum (150g), sliced thinly
300g sugar snap peas, trimmed

1 Combine sauce, rind and juice in small saucepan; bring to the boil.
Remove from heat.
2 Place noodles in large heatproof bowl; cover with boiling water,
separate with fork, drain.
3 Combine flour and five-spice in medium bowl, add tofu; toss to coat
tofu in flour mixture.
4 Heat half the oil in wok; cook tofu, in batches, until browned all over.
5 Heat remaining oil in wok; stir-fry onion, garlic and capsicum until onion
softens. Add noodles, peas and half the lemon chilli sauce; stir-fry until
peas are just tender.
6 Serve noodles topped with tofu and drizzled with remaining lemon
chilli sauce.

preparation time 15 minutes **cooking time** 25 minutes **serves** 4
nutritional count per serving 12.2g total fat (1.8g saturated fat);
2241kJ (536 cal); 80.3g carbohydrate; 24.6g protein; 8.5g fibre

Chicken and thai basil fried rice

You need to cook about 1⅓ cups (265g) jasmine rice for this recipe.

¼ cup (60ml) peanut oil
1 medium brown onion (150g), chopped finely
3 cloves garlic, crushed
2 fresh long green chillies, seeded, chopped finely
1 tablespoon brown sugar
500g chicken breast fillets, chopped coarsely
2 medium red capsicums (400g), sliced thinly
200g green beans, chopped coarsely
4 cups cooked jasmine rice
2 tablespoons fish sauce
2 tablespoons soy sauce
½ cup loosely packed fresh thai basil leaves

1 Heat oil in wok; stir-fry onion, garlic and chilli until onion softens. Add sugar; stir-fry until dissolved. Add chicken; stir-fry until lightly browned. Add capsicum and beans; stir-fry until vegetables are just tender and chicken is cooked through.
2 Add rice and sauces; stir-fry, tossing gently to combine. Remove from heat; add basil leaves, toss gently to combine.

preparation time 10 minutes **cooking time** 20 minutes **serves** 4
nutritional count per serving 20.3g total fat (4.2g saturated fat);
4473kJ (1070 cal); 173g carbohydrate; 44g protein; 5.1g fibre

Tofu, cashew and vegie stir-fry

1 tablespoon vegetable oil
1 fresh long red chilli, sliced thinly
500g packaged fresh stir-fry vegetables
400g packaged marinated tofu pieces, chopped coarsely
½ cup (75g) roasted unsalted cashews
⅓ cup (80ml) hoisin sauce
1 tablespoon lime juice

1 Heat oil in wok; stir-fry chilli, vegetables, tofu and nuts until vegetables are just tender.
2 Add sauce and juice; stir-fry until hot.

preparation time 5 minutes **cooking time** 10 minutes **serves** 4
nutritional count per serving 22.6g total fat (3.4g saturated fat);
1563kJ (374 cal); 20.9g carbohydrate; 18.2g protein; 8.4g fibre
tip we used cryovac-packed ready-to-serve sweet chilli tofu, available
from Asian food shops and some supermarkets.

Sichuan eggplant, almond and wombok stir-fry

⅓ cup (55g) blanched almonds, halved
1 tablespoon peanut oil
1 medium brown onion (150g), chopped coarsely
2 cloves garlic, crushed
1 fresh small red thai chilli, chopped finely
12 baby eggplants (720g), sliced thickly
150g snake beans, trimmed, chopped coarsely
1 small wombok (700g), trimmed, chopped coarsely
2 teaspoons sichuan peppercorns, crushed coarsely
¼ cup (60ml) vegetable stock
2 tablespoons hoisin sauce
1 tablespoon dark soy sauce
1 tablespoon red wine vinegar
½ cup loosely packed thai basil leaves
1 fresh long red chilli, sliced thinly

1 Stir-fry nuts in heated wok until browned lightly; remove from wok.
2 Heat oil in wok; stir-fry onion, garlic and thai chilli until onion softens. Add eggplant and beans; stir-fry until tender. Add wombok; stir-fry until wilted.
3 Add pepper, stock, sauces and vinegar; stir-fry until hot. Remove from heat; stir in basil. Serve sprinkled with nuts and chilli.

preparation time 15 minutes **cooking time** 20 minutes **serves** 4
nutritional count per serving 13.6g total fat (1.4g saturated); 982kJ (235cal); 13.9g carbohydrate; 9.3g protein; 10.7g fibre

Vegetable chap-chai

1 tablespoon peanut oil
1 clove garlic, crushed
4cm piece fresh ginger (20g), grated
150g tat soi, trimmed
200g choy sum, chopped coarsely
200g baby bok choy, chopped coarsely
200g wombok, chopped coarsely
150g sugar snap peas
2 tablespoons soy sauce
¼ cup (60ml) hoisin sauce

1 Heat oil in wok; stir-fry garlic and ginger until fragrant.
2 Add tat soi, choy sum, bok choy, wombok, peas and combined sauces; stir-fry until vegetables are just tender.

preparation time 10 minutes **cooking time** 10 minutes **serves** 4
nutritional count per serving 5.7g total fat (1g saturated fat);
472kJ (113 cal); 9.7g carbohydrate; 3.6g protein; 4.6g fibre

Hot, sweet and sour mixed vegetables

1 tablespoon peanut oil
3cm piece fresh ginger (15g), grated
2 cloves garlic, crushed
2 fresh small red thai chillies, chopped finely
1 medium red capsicum (200g), sliced thinly
1 medium yellow capsicum (200g), sliced thinly
230g fresh baby corn, halved lengthways
¼ cup (60ml) vegetable stock
2 tablespoons vegetarian mushroom oyster sauce
2 tablespoons grated palm sugar
2 tablespoons tamarind concentrate
350g baby buk choy, chopped coarsely
280g gai lan, chopped coarsely
150g oyster mushrooms, chopped coarsely
6 green onions, cut into 3cm lengths
½ cup firmly packed vietnamese mint leaves

1 Heat oil in wok; stir-fry ginger, garlic and chilli until fragrant. Add capsicums and corn; stir-fry until tender. Add stock, sauce, sugar and tamarind; stir-fry 2 minutes.
2 Add buk choy, gai lan and mushrooms to wok; stir-fry until greens wilt. Remove from heat; stir in onion and mint.

preparation time 20 minutes **cooking time** 10 minutes **serves** 4
nutritional count per serving 6.1g total fat (1g saturated fat);
861kJ (206 cal); 25.8g carbohydrate; 7.9g protein; 8.5g fibre

Spinach with toasted almonds

2 teaspoons peanut oil
2 tablespoons rice wine vinegar
2 tablespoons soy sauce
2 tablespoons honey
1 clove garlic, crushed
1cm piece fresh ginger (5g), grated
1kg spinach
4 green onions, chopped coarsely
½ cup (40g) flaked almonds, toasted

1 Heat oil in wok, add vinegar, sauce, honey, garlic and ginger; bring to the boil.
2 Add spinach and onion; stir-fry until spinach is just wilted. Serve sprinkled with nuts.

preparation time 5 minutes **cooking time** 10 minutes **serves** 4
nutritional count per serving 2.7g total fat (0.4g saturated fat); 426kJ (102 cal); 13.4g carbohydrate; 4g protein; 3.9g fibre

Mixed green vegetables and fried tofu

300g fresh firm silken tofu
1 tablespoon peanut oil
1 medium brown onion (150g), sliced thinly
2 cloves garlic, crushed
2cm piece fresh ginger (10g), grated
1 fresh small red thai chilli, chopped finely
340g asparagus, cut into 3cm lengths
350g broccolini, cut into 3cm lengths
200g sugar snap peas, trimmed
500g buk choy, chopped coarsely
¼ cup (60ml) vegetable stock
¼ cup (60ml) hoisin sauce
¼ cup (60ml) vegetarian mushroom oyster sauce
1 tablespoon lime juice
100g bean sprouts

1 Cut tofu into 2cm cubes; spread, in single layer, on absorbent-paper-lined tray. Cover tofu with more absorbent paper, stand 10 minutes.
2 Heat half the oil in wok; stir-fry tofu, in batches, until browned lightly.
3 Heat remaining oil in wok; stir-fry onion, garlic, ginger and chilli until onion softens. Add asparagus, broccolini and peas; stir-fry until vegetables are tender. Add buk choy, stock, sauces and juice; stir-fry until buk choy wilts.
4 Return tofu to wok; stir-fry until combined. Remove from heat; stir in sprouts.

preparation time 25 minutes **cooking time** 10 minutes **serves** 4
nutritional serving per serving 11.6g total fat (1.8g saturated fat);
1191kJ (285 cal); 18.4g carbohydrate; 20.5g protein; 12.3g fibre

Stir-fried mixed vegetables

⅓ cup (80ml) soy sauce
2 tablespoons coarsely chopped fresh coriander
1 teaspoon honey
190g fried tofu, cut into 1cm slices
6 dried shiitake mushrooms
1 tablespoon peanut oil
3 cloves garlic, crushed
2cm piece fresh ginger (10g), grated
10cm stick fresh lemon grass (20g), chopped finely
2 medium carrots (240g), cut into 6cm strips
200g snake beans, cut into 6cm lengths
500g cauliflower, cut into florets
230g can bamboo shoots, rinsed, drained
600g wombok, chopped coarsely
¾ cup (180ml) vegetable stock
1 tablespoon cornflour
2 teaspoons hoisin sauce
1 teaspoon lime juice
½ teaspoon sambal oelek

1 Combine soy sauce, coriander and honey in small bowl with tofu.
2 Place mushrooms in small heatproof bowl; cover with boiling water. Stand 20 minutes; drain. Discard stems; slice caps thinly.
3 Heat oil in wok; stir-fry garlic, ginger and lemon grass until fragrant. Add carrots, beans and cauliflower; stir-fry until vegetables are just tender.
4 Add tofu mixture to wok with bamboo shoots, mushrooms and wombok; stir-fry until heated through. Stir in blended stock, cornflour, sauce, juice and sambal; stir over heat until mixture boils and thickens slightly.

preparation time 15 minutes (plus standing time)
cooking time 10 minutes **serves** 6
nutritional count per serving 5.8g total fat (1g saturated fat); 598kJ (143 cal); 10.2g carbohydrate; 9.4g protein; 6.3g fibre

Stir-fried greens with green beans

1 tablespoon sesame oil
2 cloves garlic, crushed
2cm piece fresh ginger (10g), grated
300g green beans, halved
8 green onions, chopped coarsely
500g spinach, chopped coarsely
600g baby buk choy, chopped coarsely
2 tablespoons soy sauce
1 tablespoon sweet chilli sauce
2 tablespoons finely chopped fresh coriander

1 Heat oil in wok; stir-fry garlic, ginger, beans and onion until beans are just tender.
2 Add spinach and buk choy; stir-fry until buk choy is just wilted. Add combined sauces; stir-fry until hot. Serve sprinkled with coriander.

preparation time 10 minutes **cooking time** 10 minutes **serves** 4
nutritional count per serving 5.5g total fat (0.7g saturated fat);
464kJ (111 cal); 6.2g carbohydrate; 6g protein; 6.8g fibre

Stir-fried vegetables and tofu in black bean sauce

500g firm tofu
2 tablespoons peanut oil
6 finger eggplant (360g), quartered lengthways
1 medium red capsicum (200g), sliced thinly
230g can sliced water chestnuts, rinsed, drained
2 cloves garlic, crushed
2cm piece fresh ginger (10g), grated
250g broccolini, chopped coarsely
500g choy sum, chopped coarsely
2 tablespoons kecap manis
⅓ cup (80ml) black bean sauce

1 Weight tofu between two boards; stand, tilted, 10 minutes. Cut tofu into 2cm cubes; pat dry between layers of absorbent paper.
2 Heat half the oil in wok; stir-fry tofu, in batches, until lightly browned. Drain on absorbent paper; cover to keep warm.
3 Heat half the remaining oil in same wok; stir-fry eggplant until soft. Add capsicum and water chestnuts; stir-fry until vegetables are just tender, remove from wok.
4 Heat remaining oil in wok; stir-fry garlic and ginger until fragrant. Add broccolini and choy sum; stir-fry until choy sum just wilts. Add combined sauces and eggplant mixture; stir-fry until heated through. Add tofu; toss gently to combine.

preparation time 15 minutes (plus standing time)
cooking time 15 minutes **serves** 4
nutritional count per serving 18.8g total fat (2.9g saturated fat); 1342kJ (321 cal); 11.4g carbohydrate; 22.3g protein; 10.3g fibre

Cauliflower, pea and paneer balti

1 tablespoon sesame seeds
2 tablespoons vegetable oil
6 dried curry leaves
¼ teaspoon black mustard seeds
1 teaspoon ground coriander
1 teaspoon hot chilli powder
1 teaspoon ground cumin
2 cloves garlic, crushed
400g can diced tomatoes
1kg cauliflower, trimmed, cut into florets
½ cup (125ml) water
1 cup (120g) frozen peas
400g paneer cheese, cut into 2cm cubes
¼ cup coarsely chopped fresh coriander

1 Heat wok; roast sesame seeds until browned lightly. Remove from wok.
2 Heat oil in wok; stir-fry leaves and mustard seeds until seeds pop.
3 Add ground coriander, chilli, cumin and garlic to wok; stir-fry until fragrant. Add undrained tomatoes; simmer, stirring, about 2 minutes or until mixture thickens slightly.
4 Add cauliflower and the water; stir-fry until cauliflower is almost tender. Add peas, cheese and chopped coriander; stir-fry until hot. Remove from heat; sprinkle with sesame seeds.

preparation time 20 minutes **cooking time** 25 minutes **serves** 4
nutritional count per serving 34.9g total fat (16.7g saturated fat); 2002kJ (479 cal); 11.4g carbohydrate; 26.6g protein; 8.1g fibre
tip for this recipe, since the paneer cheese is stir-fried, haloumi makes a good substitute if paneer is not available.

Asian greens in oyster sauce

1 cup (250ml) chicken stock
⅓ cup (80ml) oyster sauce
2 teaspoons sesame oil
2kg baby buk choy, trimmed
1kg choy sum, trimmed

1 Combine stock, sauce and oil in wok; bring to the boil. Add buk choy; cook, stirring, about 3 minutes or until buk choy is slightly wilted.
2 Stir in choy sum; cook, covered, about 5 minutes or until both greens are tender and just wilted.

preparation time 5 minutes **cooking time** 10 minutes **serves** 6
nutritional count per serving 6.4g total fat (0.3g saturated fat);
418kJ (100 cal); 8.7g carbohydrate; 6.4g protein; 6.5g fibre

almonds

blanched skin removed.

flaked paper-thin slices.

slivered small pieces cut lengthways.

artichoke, hearts the tender centre of globe artichokes; harvested from the plant after its prickly choke is removed. Cooked hearts can be bought from delis or canned in brine.

bacon rashers also called bacon slices.

basil, thai also called horapa; has small leaves, purplish stems and a slight aniseed taste.

bay leaves aromatic leaves from the bay tree available fresh or dried.

beans

black-eyed also called black-eyed peas or cowpea; the dried seed of a variant of the snake or yard-long bean.

broad also called fava, windsor and horse beans; available dried, fresh, canned and frozen. Fresh should be peeled twice (discarding the outer long green pod and the beige-green tough inner shell); the frozen beans have had their pods removed but the beige shell still needs removal.

cannellini small white bean similar in flavour and appearance to other *phaseolus vulgaris* varieties (great northern, navy or haricot). Available dried or canned.

snake are long (about 40cm), thin, round, fresh green beans, Asian in origin, with a taste similar to green or french beans.

beef

eye fillet tenderloin, fillet.

rump boneless tender cut taken from the upper part of the round (hindquarter).

scotch fillet cut from the muscle running behind the shoulder along the spine. Also known as cube roll, cuts include standing rib roast and rib-eye.

beetroot or red beets.

bicarbonate of soda also called baking soda.

breadcrumbs, stale crumbs made by grating, blending or processing 1- or 2-day-old bread.

broccolini a cross between broccoli and Chinese kale; long asparagus-like stems with a long loose floret, both completely edible. Resembles broccoli in looks, but is milder and sweeter in taste.

buk choy also called bok choy, pak choi or chinese white cabbage; has a fresh, mild mustard taste. Both stems and leaves are cooked.

burghul also called bulghur wheat; hulled steamed wheat kernels, once dried, are crushed into various sized grains.

butter we use salted butter unless stated otherwise.

buttermilk originally the term given to the slightly sour liquid left after butter was churned from cream, today it made similarly to yogurt. Sold alongside fresh milk products in supermarkets. Despite the implication of its name, it is low in fat.

caperberries olive-sized fruit formed after the buds of the caper bush have flowered; they are usually sold pickled in a vinegar brine with stalks intact.

capers the grey-green buds of a Mediterranean shrub, sold either dried and salted or pickled in a vinegar brine.

capsicum also called pepper or bell pepper.

cardamom a spice native to India and used extensively in its cuisine; can be purchased in pod, seed or ground form. Has an aromatic, sweetly rich flavour.

cashews plump, kidney-shaped, golden-brown nuts with a sweet, buttery flavour; contains 48% fat so should be stored in the refrigerator to avoid becoming rancid. We use roasted unsalted cashews.

char siu sauce also called chinese barbecue sauce; a dark-red-brown paste-like ingredient with a sharp sweet and spicy flavour. Made with fermented soybeans, honey and various spices.

cheese

bocconcini from the diminutive of "boccone", meaning mouthful in Italian; walnut-sized, baby mozzarella, a delicate, semi-soft, white cheese traditionally made from buffalo milk. Sold fresh, it spoils rapidly; store refrigerated in brine, for 1 or 2 days at the most.

fetta Greek in origin; a crumbly textured goat- or sheep-milk cheese with a sharp, salty taste.

haloumi a Greek Cypriot cheese with a semi-firm, spongy texture and very salty yet sweet flavour. It's best grilled or fried, and holds its shape well on being heated. Best eaten while warm as it becomes tough and rubbery on cooling.

mozzarella soft, spun-curd, cow-milk cheese; it is the most popular pizza cheese because of its low melting point and elasticity when heated.

paneer a simple, delicate fresh cheese. Available in cryovac-packs in some supermarkets or loose, in brine, in Indian food shops. Replace with ricotta if hard to find.

parmesan also called parmigiano; a hard, grainy cow-milk cheese. The curd is salted in brine for a month then aged for up to 2 years.

ricotta a soft, sweet, moist, white cow-milk cheese, low in fat and slightly grainy in texture. Its name roughly translates as "cooked again" and refers to its manufacture from a whey that is itself a by-product of other cheese making.

chicken

breast fillet breast halved, skinned and boned.

thigh fillet thigh with skin and centre bone removed.

chickpeas also called garbanzos; an irregularly round legume. Available canned or dried (soak in cold water for several hours before use).

chilli

chipotle pronounced cheh-pote-lay, is the name given to jalapeño chillies once they've been dried and smoked. Has a deep, intensely smoky flavour rather than a searing heat; rehydrate before use.

jalapeño pronounced hah-lah-pain-yo. Fairly hot, medium-sized, plump, dark green chilli; available pickled, canned or bottled, and fresh, from greengrocers.

red thai also known as "scuds"; tiny, very hot.

chinese barbecued

duck dipped into and brushed during roasting with a sticky sweet coating made from soy sauce, sherry, ginger, five-spice, star anise and hoisin sauce. Available from Asian food shops.

chinese barbecued

pork roasted pork fillet with a sweet, sticky coating. Available from Asian food shops.

chinese cooking

wine also called hao hsing or chinese rice wine; made from fermented rice, wheat, sugar and salt with a 13.5% alcohol content. Inexpensive and found in Asian food shops; if you can't find it, replace with mirin or sherry.

chorizo sausage

Spanish in origin, made of coarsely ground pork and highly seasoned with garlic and chilli.

choy sum

also called pakaukeo or flowering cabbage, a member of the buk choy family; has long stems, light green leaves and yellow flowers. Both stems and leaves are edible.

coconut

cream obtained from the first pressing of the coconut flesh alone. Available in cans and cartons at supermarkets.

milk the diluted liquid from the second pressing of the white flesh of a mature coconut (not the liquid inside). Available in cans and cartons at most supermarkets.

shredded unsweetened thin strips of dried coconut flesh.

coriander

also called cilantro or chinese parsley; bright-green-leafed herb with a pungent aroma and taste.

Both stems and roots are used: wash well before chopping. Coriander seeds are dried and sold whole or ground; neither form tastes remotely like the fresh leaf.

cornflour also known as cornstarch.

couscous a fine, grain-like cereal product made from semolina. A semolina flour and water dough is sieved then dehydrated to produce minuscule even-sized pellets of couscous; it is rehydrated by steaming or by adding warm liquid. Swells to three or four times its original size.

cranberries available dried and frozen; have a rich, astringent flavour and can be used in sweet or savoury dishes. The dried version can usually be substituted for or with other dried fruit.

cumin is the dried seed of a plant related to the parsley family. Has a spicy, almost curry-like flavour. Available dried as seeds or ground.

curly endive also called frisée; prickly-looking, curly-leafed green vegetable with an edible white heart. Fairly bitter in flavour; used in salads.

eggplant also called aubergine.

fennel also called finocchio or anise; a crunchy green vegetable slightly resembling celery.

fish sauce called naam pla if Thai-made, nuoc

naam if Vietnamese; the two are almost identical. Made from pulverised salted fermented fish; has a pungent smell and strong taste. Use according to your taste.

five-spice powder ingredients vary, but are usually a blend of cloves, ground cinnamon, star anise, sichuan pepper and fennel seeds. Found in most supermarkets or Asian food shops.

gai lan also called gai larn, chinese broccoli and chinese kale; green vegetable used more for its stems than its leaves.

galangal a root, similar to ginger in its use. It has a hot-sour ginger-citrusy flavour.

ginger

fresh called green or root ginger; thick gnarled root of a tropical plant.

pickled pink or red coloured; available, packaged, from Asian food shops. Paper-thin shavings of ginger in a mixture of vinegar, sugar and natural colouring.

hoisin sauce a thick, sweet and spicy chinese barbecue sauce made from salted fermented soy beans, onions and garlic. Available from supermarkets and Asian food shops.

kaffir lime leaves also called bai magrood; looks like two glossy dark green leaves joined end to end to form a rounded hourglass shape. Sold

fresh, dried or frozen; dried leaves are less potent so double the number if using them instead of fresh; a strip of fresh lime peel can replace each kaffir leaf.

kecap manis a dark, thick sweet soy sauce. Its sweetness is derived from the addition of molasses or palm sugar.

kumara the polynesian name of an orange-fleshed sweet potato often confused with yam.

lamb, backstrap also called eye of loin; the larger fillet from a row of loin chops or cutlets.

lemon grass a tall, clumping, lemon-tasting and smelling, sharp-edged tropical grass; the white lower part of the stem is used, finely chopped. Available in Asian food shops and supermarkets.

lentils dried pulses identified and named after their colour (red, brown, yellow).

french green a local cousin to the famous (and very expensive) French lentils du puy; green-blue, tiny lentils with a nutty, earthy flavour and a hardy nature that allows them to be rapidly cooked without disintegrating.

lettuce

butter small, round, loosely formed heads with a sweet flavour; soft, buttery-textured leaves range from pale green on the outer leaves to pale yellow-green inner leaves.

coral very curly and tightly furled leaves that do look like coral; comes in distinctive tasting red and green leaves.

cos also called romaine; the traditional caesar salad lettuce. Long, with leaves ranging from dark green on the outside to almost white near the core; the leaves have a stiff centre rib giving a slight cupping effect.

mizuna Japanese in origin; the frizzy green salad leaves have a delicate mustard flavour.

oak leaf also called feuille de chene; curly-leafed but not as frizzy as the coral lettuce. Found in both red and green varieties.

radicchio Italian in origin; a member of the chicory family. The dark burgundy leaves and strong, bitter flavour can be cooked or eaten raw.

rocket also called arugula, rugula and rucola; peppery green leaf eaten raw in salads or used in cooking. Baby rocket leaves are smaller and less peppery.

macadamias fairly large, slightly soft, buttery rich nut. Store in the fridge to prevent their high oil content turning them rancid.

maple syrup distilled from the sap of sugar maple trees found only in Canada and about ten states in the USA. Maple-flavoured syrup or pancake syrup is not an adequate substitute for the real thing.

mirin a Japanese champagne-coloured cooking wine, made of glutinous rice and alcohol. It is used just for cooking and should not be confused with sake.

miso fermented soy bean paste. Generally, the darker the miso, the saltier the taste and denser the texture. Buy in tubs or plastic packs.

mushrooms

button small, cultivated white mushrooms with a mild flavour.

oyster also known as abalone; grey-white mushrooms shaped like a fan. Prized for their smooth texture and subtle, oyster-like flavour.

shiitake *fresh*, are also called chinese black, forest or golden oak mushrooms. Although cultivated, they have the earthiness and taste of wild mushrooms. *dried* also called donko or dried chinese mushrooms. Uniquely meaty in flavour; rehydrate before use.

swiss brown also called roman or cremini. Light to dark brown in colour with full-bodied flavour.

mustard

dijon also called french; pale brown, creamy, distinctively flavoured, mild French mustard.

seeds available in black (also called brown) and white (also called yellow seeds). Black seeds are more pungent than white.

wholegrain also called seeded. A French-style coarse-grain mustard made from crushed mustard seeds and dijon-style french mustard.

noodles

fresh egg also called ba mee or yellow noodles; made from wheat flour and eggs, sold fresh or dried. Range in size from very fine strands to wide, spaghetti-like pieces as thick as a shoelace.

fried deep-fried crispy egg noodles packaged in 50g or 100g packets.

hokkien also called stir-fry noodles; fresh wheat noodles resembling thick, yellow-brown spaghetti. No need no pre-cooking.

rice stick also called sen lek, ho fun or kway teow; come in different widths (thin for soups, wide for stir-fries), but all should be soaked in hot water to soften.

rice vermicelli also called sen mee, mei fun or bee hoon. Used in spring rolls and cold salads. Before use, soak in hot water until softened, boil briefly then rinse with hot water.

soba thin, pale-brown Japanese noodle; made from buckwheat and wheat flour. Available dried, fresh and flavoured (such as green tea).

oil

cooking spray we use a cholesterol-free spray made from canola oil.

olive made from ripened olives. *Extra virgin* and *virgin* are the first and second press, respectively and are considered the best; reference to "extra light" or "light" is to taste not fat levels.

peanut pressed from ground peanuts; most commonly used in Asian cooking because of its high smoke point.

sesame made from toasted, crushed, white sesame seeds.

vegetable any oil sourced from plants.

onions

fried shallots served as a condiment. Found in cellophane bags or jars at Asian food shops.

green also called scallion or (incorrectly) shallot; an immature onion picked before the bulb has formed, having a long, bright-green edible stalk.

purple shallots also called asian shallots; related to the onion but resembes garlic. Thin-layered and intensely flavoured.

red also called spanish, red spanish or bermuda onion; a sweet-flavoured, large, purple-red onion.

spring crisp, narrow green-leafed tops and a round sweet white bulb larger than green onions.

oyster sauce thick, richly flavoured brown sauce made from oysters and their brine, cooked with salt and soy sauce, and thickened.

pancetta an Italian unsmoked bacon.

paprika ground dried sweet red capsicum.

pecans native to the USA; are golden brown, buttery and rich.

pepitas the pale green kernels of dried pumpkin seeds; can be bought plain or salted.

pine nuts also called pignoli; not a nut but the small, cream-coloured kernel from pine cones.

pomegranate dark-red, leathery-skinned fresh fruit about the size of an orange filled with hundreds of seeds, each wrapped in an edible lucent-crimson pulp having a unique tangy sweet-sour flavour.

potato, kipfler small, finger-shaped, nutty flavour.

rice

jasmine a perfumed long-grained white rice; moist in texture, it clings together after cooking.

wild blend a pre-made mixture of white long-grain and wild rice.

sake made from fermented rice; is used for marinating, cooking and as part of dipping sauces. Use dry sherry, brandy or vermouth if sake is unavailable.

sambal oelek also ulek or olek; Indonesian in origin, this is a salty paste made from ground chillies and vinegar.

savoy cabbage large, heavy head with crinkled dark-green outer leaves; a mild tasting cabbage.

shrimp paste a strong-scented, very firm preserved paste made of salted dried shrimp. Used sparingly, it should be chopped, then foil-wrapped and roasted before use.

sichuan peppercorns also called szechuan or chinese pepper, native to the Sichuan province of China. A mildly hot spice from the prickly ash tree. Is not related to the peppercorn family, but its small, red-brown aromatic berries look like black peppercorns and have a distinctive peppery-lemon flavour and aroma.

silver beet also called swiss chard and incorrectly, spinach; has fleshy stalks and large leaves.

soy sauce made from fermented soybeans. Several variations (dark, light) are available in Asian food shops and supermarkets; we use Japanese soy sauce unless stated otherwise.

spinach also known as english spinach and incorrectly, silver beet. Baby spinach leaves are best eaten raw in salads;

larger leaves should be added last and cooked until barely wilted.

sugar

brown an extremely soft, fine granulated sugar; retains molasses for its characteristic colour and flavour.

palm also called nam tan pip, jaggery, jawa or gula melaka; made from the sap of the sugar palm tree. Light brown to black in colour and usually sold in rock-hard cakes; brown sugar can be used instead.

tamarind the tamarind tree produces clusters of hairy brown pods, each of which is filled with seeds and a viscous pulp, that are dried and pressed into the blocks of tamarind found in Asian food shops. Gives a sweet-sour, slightly astringent taste to marinades, pastes, sauces and dressings.

tat soi also called pak choy, rosette and chinese flat cabbage; a member of the same family as buk choy, it has the same mild flavour. Its dark-green leaves are usually eaten in salads.

tofu

firm made by compressing bean curd to remove most of the water. Good used in stir-fries as it can be tossed without disintegrating. Can also be flavoured, preserved in rice wine or brine.

fried packaged pieces of deep-fried soft bean curd; the surface is brown and crunchy and the inside quite dry.

silken not a type of tofu but reference to the manufacturing process of straining soybean liquid through silk; this denotes best quality.

turmeric also known as kamin; is a rhizome related to galangal and ginger. Must be grated or pounded to release its somewhat acrid aroma and pungent flavour. Known for the golden colour it imparts, fresh turmeric can be substituted with the more commonly found dried powder.

vietnamese mint not a mint at all, but a pungent and peppery narrow-leafed member of the buckwheat family.

vinegar

apple cider made from fermented apples.

balsamic originally from Modena, Italy, there are now many on the market ranging in pungency and quality depending on how, and for how long, they have been aged. Quality is determined up to a point by price; use the most expensive sparingly.

raspberry made from fresh raspberries steeped in white wine vinegar.

rice a colourless vinegar made from fermented rice and flavoured with

sugar and salt. Also called seasoned rice vinegar; use sherry instead.

walnuts as well as being a good source of fibre and healthy oils, nuts contain a range of vitamins, minerals and other beneficial plant components called phytochemicals. Each type of nut has a special make-up and walnuts contain the beneficial omega-3 fatty acids.

wasabi an Asian horseradish used to make the pungent, green-coloured sauce; sold as powder or paste.

watercress member of the cress family, a large group of peppery greens; highly perishable, it must be used soon after purchase.

witlof also called belgian endive; related to and confused with chicory. Grown in darkness like white asparagus to prevent it becoming green; looks somewhat like a tightly furled, cream to very light-green cigar.

wombok also called chinese cabbage, peking or napa cabbage; elongated in shape with pale green, crinkly leaves.

worcestershire sauce thin, dark-brown spicy sauce developed by the British when in India.

yogurt we use plain full-cream yogurt unless stated otherwise.

index

MEASURES

One Australian metric measuring cup holds approximately 250ml, one Australian metric tablespoon holds 20ml, one Australian metric teaspoon holds 5ml.

The difference between one country's measuring cups and another's is within a two- or three-teaspoon variance, and will not affect your cooking results.North America, New Zealand and the United Kingdom use a 15ml tablespoon.

All cup and spoon measurements are level. The most accurate way of measuring dry ingredients is to weigh them. When measuring liquids, use a clear glass or plastic jug with the metric markings.

We use large eggs with an average weight of 60g.

LIQUID MEASURES

METRIC	IMPERIAL
30ml	1 fluid oz
60ml	2 fluid oz
100ml	3 fluid oz
125ml	4 fluid oz
150ml	5 fluid oz (¼ pint/1 gill)
190ml	6 fluid oz
250ml	8 fluid oz
300ml	10 fluid oz (½ pint)
500ml	16 fluid oz
600ml	20 fluid oz (1 pint)
1000ml (1 litre)	1¾ pints

LENGTH MEASURES

METRIC	IMPERIAL
3mm	⅛in
6mm	¼in
1cm	½in
2cm	¾in
2.5cm	1in
5cm	2in
6cm	2½in
8cm	3in
10cm	4in
13cm	5in
15cm	6in
18cm	7in
20cm	8in
23cm	9in
25cm	10in
28cm	11in
30cm	12in (1ft)

DRY MEASURES

METRIC	IMPERIAL
15g	½oz
30g	1oz
60g	2oz
90g	3oz
125g	4oz (¼lb)
155g	5oz
185g	6oz
220g	7oz
250g	8oz (½lb)
280g	9oz
315g	10oz
345g	11oz
375g	12oz (¾lb)
410g	13oz
440g	14oz
470g	15oz
500g	16oz (1lb)
750g	24oz (1½lb)
1kg	32oz (2lb)

OVEN TEMPERATURES

These oven temperatures are only a guide for conventional ovens.
For fan-forced ovens, check the manufacturer's manual.

	°C (CELSIUS)	°F (FAHRENHEIT)	GAS MARK
Very slow	120	250	½
Slow	150	275 – 300	1 – 2
Moderately slow	160	325	3
Moderate	180	350 – 375	4 – 5
Moderately hot	200	400	6
Hot	220	425 – 450	7 – 8
Very hot	240	475	9

General manager Christine Whiston
Editorial director Susan Tomnay
Creative director Hieu Chi Nguyen
Editor Stephanie Kistner
Designer Caryl Wiggins
Food director Pamela Clark
Recipe consultant Louise Patniotis
Associate food editor Alex Somerville
Nutritional information Belinda Farlow
Director of sales Brian Cearnes
Marketing manager Bridget Cody
Business analyst Rebecca Varela
Operations manager David Scotto
Production manager Victoria Jefferys
International rights enquiries Laura Bamford
lbamford@acpuk.com

ACP Books are published by ACP Magazines
a division of PBL Media Pty Limited
Group publisher, Women's lifestyle Pat Ingram
Director of sales, Women's lifestyle Lynette Phillips
Commercial manager, Women's lifestyle Seymour Cohen
Marketing director, Women's lifestyle Matthew Dominello
Public relations manager, Women's lifestyle Hannah Deveraux
Creative director, Events, Women's lifestyle Luke Bonnano
Research Director, Women's lifestyle Justin Stone
ACP Magazines, Chief Executive officer Scott Lorson
PBL Media, Chief Executive officer Ian Law

Produced by ACP Books, Sydney
Published by ACP Books, a division of ACP Magazines Ltd.
54 Park St, Sydney NSW Australia 2000. GPO Box 4088, Sydney, NSW 2001.
Phone +61 2 9282 8618 Fax +61 2 9267 9438
acpbooks@acpmagazines.com.au www.acpbooks.com.au
Printed by Toppan Printing Co., China.

Australia Distributed by Network Services, GPO Box 4088, Sydney, NSW 2001.
Phone +61 2 9282 8777 Fax +61 2 9264 3278
networkweb@networkservicescompany.com.au
United Kingdom Distributed by Australian Consolidated Press (UK),
10 Scirocco Close, Moulton Park Office Village, Northampton, NN3 6AP.
Phone +44 1604 642 200 Fax +44 1604 642 300
books@acpuk.com www.acpuk.com
New Zealand Distributed by Netlink Distribution Company, ACP Media Centre,
Cnr Fanshawe and Beaumont Streets, Westhaven, Auckland. PO Box 47906, Ponsonby, Auckland, NZ.
Phone +64 9 366 9966 Fax 0800 277 412 ask@ndc.co.nz
South Africa Distributed by PSD Promotions, 30 Diesel Road Isando, Gauteng Johannesburg.
PO Box 1175, Isando 1600, Gauteng Johannesburg.
Phone +27 11 392 6065/6/7 Fax +27 11 392 6079/80 orders@psdprom.co.za
Canada Distributed by Publishers Group Canada
Order Desk & Customer Service 9050 Shaughnessy Street, Vancouver BC V6P 6E5
Phone (800) 663 5714 Fax (800) 565 3770 service@raincoast.com

Title: Toss: the Australian women's weekly/food director, Pamela Clark; editor, Stephanie Kistner
Publisher: Sydney: ACP Books, 2008
ISBN: 978-1-86396-755-6 (pbk)
Notes: Includes index
Subjects: Salads
Other authors/contributors: Clark, Pamela; Kistner, Stephanie
Dewey number: 641.83
© ACP Magazines Ltd 2008
ABN 18 053 273 546

To order books, phone 136 116 (within Australia).
Send recipe enquiries to: askpamela@acpmagazines.com.au

Front cover Salade niçoise, page 94
Front cover photographer Rob Palmer
Front cover stylist Jane Hann
Front cover food preparation Ariarne Bradshaw
Illustrations Hannah Blackmore
Back cover photographer Brett Stevens
Back cover stylist David Morgan